Viktor Frankl
Recollections

An Autobiography

Viktor Frankl
Recollections
An Autobiography

VIKTOR E. FRANKL
Author, *Man's Search for Meaning*

Translated by
Joseph Fabry and Judith Fabry

Foreword by
Joseph Fabry

PERSEUS PUBLISHING
Cambridge, Massachusetts

Many of the designations used by manufacturers and sellers to distinguish their products are claimed as trademarks. Where those designations appear in this book and Perseus Publishing was aware of a trademark claim, the designations have been printed in initial capital letters.

A CIP catalog record for this book is available from the Library of Congress. ISBN: 0–7382–0355-6

Perseus Publishing is a member of the Perseus Books Group

The original version of this volume was published in German under the title *Was nicht in meinen Büchern steht,* as was the second edition, both © 1995 Psychologie Verlags Union, Weinheim, Germany.

1 2 3 4 5 6 7 8 9 10—03 02 01 00 99
First paperback printing, June 2000

Perseus Publishing books are available at special discounts for bulk purchases in the U.S. by corporations, institutions, and other organizations. For more information, please contact the Special Markets Department at HarperCollins Publishers, 10 East 53rd Street, New York, NY 10022, or call 1–212–207–7528.

Find Perseus Publishing on the World Wide Web at
http://www.perseuspublishing.com

Frankl in 1954, from an oil painting by Florian Jakowitsch.

Foreword

I became acquainted with Dr. Viktor Frankl, as many have, through his book *Man's Search for Meaning*. When I read it in 1963, I resonated to it. I, too, had lost in the Holocaust much that had been meaningful to me—family, friends, country, career, and my language, which to me as a writer was especially painful. The book offered answers for which I had groped for 25 years. I also realized the importance of logotherapy and its philosophy for many Americans. Their lives, too, had been emptied of meaning, though for different reasons. Families were scattered because of divorce, children moving out early, grandparents living alone, careers were interrupted by the breadwinner being transferred to a more remunerative job half across the country, if not the world. Many careers had become meaningless in a society that treasured riches and pleasures above all.

At that time I was in charge of adult-education programs at the Unitarian Church of Berkeley, and wanted to make Dr. Frankl's ideas a topic of my classes. I wrote to him in Vienna, and it so happened that he was scheduled to speak at the University of California in Berkeley. We met briefly and he promised to send me "some material." During the course of the next few weeks I received some 20 books, articles, and leaflets, all in German, my mother tongue. The more I read, the more I became convinced that a book for the intelligent American lay reader was urgently needed. It existed in neither German or English.

Dr. Frankl agreed that a general introduction to logotherapy was needed, and for the next two years a trans-Atlantic correspondence course in logotherapy ensued. We tried various approaches: my translating a book he was to write, my ghostwriting it, a book in dialogue form—nothing worked. He never wanted to say anything favorable about his work because, he didn't want to praise himself. Nor did he want to say anything unfavorable because, as he said, "I have enough critics, I do not need to criticize myself." Finally he suggested I write the book myself. "Then you can praise and blame me as much as you want," he said.

The book, *The Pursuit of Meaning*, was published in 1968 and changed my life. I took early retirement from my editorship at the University of California and became a logotherapist, arranging sharing groups. This was my way of finding the logotherapeutic secret to successful retirement. You don't retire *from* a job (which may have become stale) but *to* an activity that is meaningful to you.

The contact between Berkeley and Vienna remained constant. I was privileged to drive Dr. Frankl to his various commitments during his California visits. I saw many instances of how he *lived* logotherapy and its principles, of which he writes in his books. At the conclusion of one of his lectures, an official of nearby San Quentin prison passed on to Dr. Frankl a request of a prisoner who had read *Man's Search for Meaning* in the prison library and, having heard of Dr. Frankl being in the neighborhood, asked if he could speak to him in person. To the consternation of all who had painstakingly arranged Dr. Frankl's schedule of lectures, interviews, and conferences, he immediately agreed to see the man. It was a lesson to me of what he means by fulfilling the meaning of the moment, especially when you are in a unique position to do a certain task.

Another time my wife and I walked with the Frankls on the Alpine mountain where they did their climbing. When they came down again to our horizontal level, we passed a barbecue, and he remarked that burning wood always reminded him of the concentration camp because the primitive iron stoves in the barracks were heated with wood. I asked him if the memory was painful. "Oh no," he replied. "When we returned from a day of hard labor in the freezing cold, we smelled wood fire. This meant a few hours of rest." An illustration of his therapeutic advice is to find a positive angle even in painful experiences.

My work with logotherapy convinced me that it was time for Dr. Frankl to establish an institute for training and information. He refused, again with the argument that he did not want to "blow his own horn." And again he challenged me: "Why don't *you* do it?" So, in 1977, I started the Institute of Logotherapy in Berkeley although I had no administrative experience. But scores of enthusiastic volunteers helped me to establish the Institute, the oldest of 26 national institutes and societies existing all over the world.

My acquaintance (I almost dare say, friendship) with Dr. Frankl has given me precious insights into his personality, some of which he has shared with the general reader in this book. I know several facets of his intricate personality.

On his American tours, he is always under pressure from people who want to see him, interview him, confer with him. He is very jealous of time, refuses all chitchat over a cup of coffee, and does not even take time for a leisurely meal in a restaurant.

In his hometown, Vienna, Frankl is a different man. He still is rushed because he insists on answering his voluminous mail himself. But he does take time to enjoy life and experiences the meanings of the moment as he sees them. Once, my wife and I walked with him through the streets of Vienna, and he suddenly grabbed our arms and pulled us into a coffee shop. "Smell!" he ordered. "Freshly-ground Viennese coffee." A few steps later he pulled us into a bakery. "Smell," he said again, "freshly-baked Viennese rolls." He enjoys the continuous stream of logotherapists who visit him. One summer afternoon we were joined in his living room by visitors from five countries—Austria, Germany, Poland, Mexico, and the United States.

The third Viktor Frankl is Frankl on the mountaintop. For many years, every weekend he and his wife Elly drove to the Rax Mountain where they had their private room in a mountain inn. There he was surrounded by mountain guides, other rock climbers, and guests. Some knew him but most of them saw only a little old man who insisted on climbing a vertical rock to get to a plateau that easily could be reached by a winding but comfortable path. On the mountain, Frankl is relaxed, jokes with the guides in their hardly understandable dialect, and takes his time eating and chatting with strangers.

My wife and I spent many a weekend with the Frankls on that mountain top. During the midday rush, in the open-air snack hut where people were drinking beer and eating sausages, Frankl often helped the overburdened waiter clear the tables of beer glasses. One day when he was making his way to the kitchen with an armful of empty glasses, we saw a young girl asking for his autograph. He put down the glasses and obliged.

But most of the guests don't know him. Once, when he was clearing the tables, one of the guests asked him to bring him another beer. Frankl went to the kitchen and brought the beer. The guest paid him and gave him a tip. When Frankl hesitated, the guests said, "Come on, you deserve it, you have such a nice smile." When Frankl later tried to pass on the tip to the waiter, the waiter refused. "You earned it," he said. Frankl did not want to keep the tip, and neither did the waiter. They made a deal, and so it happened that the Institute of Logotherapy received a contribution of 35 cents.

There is another Frankl, and that is Frankl the prophet. He is a prophet in the Biblical sense—not to predict the future but to warn against its horrors. The horrors Frankl is warning against are the horrors of a meaningless life, an empty or frustrated life. He is not only warning against such a life but has developed his logotherapy to prevent it.

Behind his philosophy stands a very human man. We must be grateful that he now has revealed some bits of his humanness in this book.

Joseph Fabry
Berkeley, California

Preface

Witness of the twentieth century, founder of his own school of psychotherapy, and symbol for the incomprehensible—survival in the Nazi concentration camps: All of this is Viktor E. Frankl. Born in Vienna, Austria, in 1905, he looks back on almost an entire century that he shared as witness, as sufferer, and, through his life's work, as shaper.

On the occasion of his 90th birthday, March 26, 1995, we present these recollections from his life. Originally not intended for publication, Viktor Frankl over the years has written about key events in his life. To date almost nothing but his scientific writings is available, so he has decided to publish these personal encounters and events as his 31st book in German. The character of these life memories in his own words has been retained intentionally, allowing a vivid picture of one of the truly great intellectual personalities of this century.

This book came into being through close cooperation with the publisher. Viktor Frankl worked on the manuscript with undiminished vigor, despite his age and health problems, so that it would be possible to have the book ready for his 90th birthday.

Therefore, our thanks go in the first place to his wife, Elly Frankl, who not only typed the manuscript, but supported her husband in every phase of the task. Further thanks are due to Harald Mori, who was of great service in the preparation of this book. Special thanks, of course, to the author himself, who made it possible.

Martina Gast-Gampe
Munich, Germany

A Note from the Editor

This book was originally published in German to coincide with Viktor Frankl's 90th birthday in March 1995. We now present an English translation of the second edition of this work, under the title *Viktor Frankl – Recollections: An Autobiography.*

We would like to thank Joseph and Judith Fabry, who have ably translated the text from German into English. Joseph Fabry is himself an emigré from central Europe, with an intimate knowledge of the atmosphere in Vienna between the two World Wars; he has great expertise in the writing, editing, and translation of German, and in particular Austrian, literature; and last but not least, he has been a close friend of Viktor Frankl for decades.

Thanks also to Haddon Klingberg, who helped in the final editing of the translated manuscript; he provided an American scholar's and writer's feel for the hues and nuances of the English language; his acquaintance with Viktor Frankl dates back to 1963, when as a student he attended Frankl's famous Wednesday lectures at the Vienna Policlinic.

Also, a big thank you to Franz Vesely, with whom I have worked previously. Franz is the son-in-law of Viktor Frankl and was responsible for bringing this project to my attention.

Joanna Lawrence
Insight Books

Contents

Wedding picture of Frankl's parents (1901).

My Mother and Father

My mother was a descendant of an old, established Prague patrician family. The German writer Oskar Wiener,[1] who was immortalized as a character in Gustav Meyrink's[2] *Der Golem*, was her uncle. I saw him perish, long after he had become blind, in the concentration camp Theresienstadt. Also among the ancestors of my mother was Rashi,[3] who lived in the twelfth century; and "Maharal,"[4] the famous "High Rabbi Löw" of Prague. All of this I learned from a family tree that I once had occasion to see.

I almost was born in the famous Siller coffeehouse in Vienna. There my mother felt the first labor pains, on the beautiful spring afternoon of March 26, 1905. My birthday coincides with the day Beethoven died; on this point a schoolmate once commented mischievously: "One mishap comes seldom alone."

My mother was a kindhearted and deeply pious woman. I cannot understand why I was such a "pest" as a child, as I was told. As a little boy I insisted on falling asleep only when she sang to me the cradle song, "Long, Long Ago." The words did not matter to me then, and later she told me that she often sang it this way: "Keep quiet, you little pest—long, long ago, long ago." Only the melody had to be right.

I was so emotionally attached to my parental home that I suffered terrible homesickness during the first weeks and months, even years, when I had to stay overnight in the various hospitals where I was working. I wanted to spend my nights at home, not less than once a week at first, then once a month whenever possible. Later I wanted to be at home again at least on every birthday.

Tomb of the legendary Rabbi Löw at the old Jewish cemetery in Prague.

After father died in the Theresienstadt camp, and I was left alone with mother, I made it my practice to kiss her wherever I met her and whenever I said goodbye to her. This was to be sure that, should we be separated, we had always parted in peace.

And when the time had come, and I was to be deported to the Auschwitz death camp with my first wife, Tilly, I said farewell to my dear mother. At that last mo-

Frankl's mother Elsa—in the fashion of her days.

ment I asked mother, "Please give me your blessing." I can never forget how she cried out, from deep within her heart: "Yes! Yes, I bless you!"—and then she gave me her blessing. This was only about a week before she herself was deported to Auschwitz, and sent directly to the gas chamber.

In Auschwitz I thought very often of mother. Each time I fantasized how it would be when I would see her again. Naturally, I imagined that the only thing for me to do would be to kneel down and, as the expression goes, kiss the hem of her dress.

While I characterized mother as kindhearted and deeply pious, I would say that father's temperament was different. His personal philosophy was Spartan, and he had a strong sense of duty. He had principles, and he remained faithful to them. I also am a perfectionist, and this I learned from him. On Friday evenings, my older brother and I were forced by father to read a prayer in Hebrew. When we made mistakes, which happened most of the time, we were not punished, but there was no reward. But each time we read the text without mistakes, the reward was 10 heller. But this happened only a few times in a given year.

Father's philosophy could be called not only Spartan, but also stoic, had he not tended to be hot-tempered. In a fit of anger he once broke an alpine walking stick as he hit me with it. Despite this, to me he was always the personification of justice. And he always provided us with a sense of security.

For the most part, I take after my father. The characteristics I inherited from him, together with those from mother, may help to explain the tension in my personality traits. I once was given the Rorschach inkblot test by a psychologist at an Innsbruck psychiatric clinic. He claimed that he had never seen such a range between rationality and deep emotions. The former I probably inherited from father, and the latter from mother.

Father's family came from southern Moravia, which then was part of the Austro-Hungarian monarchy. As the penniless son of a master bookbinder, my father nearly

Frankl's father Gabriel as a high school student, about 1879.

starved himself through high school and into the beginning of medical school. Ultimately, he had to drop out of
medical studies for financial reasons.

Father entered public service and was able to advance to the position of director in the government's
Ministry of Social Service. Prior to his death at Theresienstadt from starvation and pneumonia, this "*Herr Direk-*

tor" once was seen scraping potato peelings from a nearly empty trash can. Later I was transferred from Theresienstadt to the camp at Kaufering, where we suffered terribly from starvation, and it was there that I came to understand my father better. Now it was I who scraped a tiny piece of carrot from the icy soil—with my fingernails.

For a time father was private secretary to government Minister Joseph Maria von Bärnreither.[5] This official wrote a book about prison reform and about his personal experiences in America. It was on his estate in Bohemia that he dictated the manuscript for this book to my father, who had been parliament stenographer for ten years.

The minister was puzzled that father always evaded the meals when he was invited. One day the minister asked him for the reason. Father explained that he ate only kosher food (and this remained the practice of our family up to World War I). Upon hearing this, Minister Bärnreither sent his coachman twice a day to a nearby village to get kosher food, so that father would not have to live only on bread, butter, and cheese.

In the department where father worked for a time was a section chief who asked him to take the minutes of a meeting. Father declined because it was the high Jewish holy day, Yom Kippur—a day of fasting and of prayers when, of course, work is forbidden. The section chief threatened father with a disciplinary investigation. Even in the face of this threat, father declined to work on this Jewish holiday and was disciplined.

Father was religious, but not without critical thoughts. He might have become the first liberal Jew in Austria, a forerunner of what later came to be called "reformed Judaism" in America. I have already written

Frankl's parents during World War II.

about his principles, but I need to expand on what I said about his stoicism. As we marched together from the train station at Bauschowitz to the Theresienstadt camp, father had his possessions in a large hat box that he carried on his back. While others were close to panic, he smiled as he told them again and again: "Be of good cheer, for God is near."

It is likely that father's ancestors came from Alsace-Lorraine. As I heard the story, during Napoleon's campaign his troops marched into the village where my father later was born. It is in southern Moravia, halfway between Vienna and Brünn, and Napoleon's grenadiers were quartered there. One of the soldiers asked a girl on the street about a local family to whom he was bringing greetings from Alsace-Lorraine. It happened that the family was the girl's own, and the soldier asked to be billeted in their home. Then he told them that he was from Alsace-Lorraine, but that one of his ancestors had emigrated from this very Moravian village some time around 1760.

Among the few things I was able to smuggle into Theresienstadt was a vial of morphine. When my father was dying from pulmonary edema, and struggling for air as he neared death, I injected him with the morphine to ease his suffering. He was then 81 years old and starving. Nevertheless, it took a second pneumonia to bring about his death.

I asked him: "Do you still have pain?"

"No."

"Do you have any wish?"

"No."

"Do you want to tell me anything?"

"No."

I kissed him and left. I knew I would not see him alive again. But I had the most wonderful feeling one can imagine. I had done what I could. I had stayed in Vienna because of my parents, and now I had accompanied father to the threshold and had spared him the unnecessary agony of death.

When mother was in mourning, the Czech Rabbi Ferda, who had known father, visited her in the camp. I was present when Ferda, comforting mother, told her that father had been a "Zaddik"—a just man. This confirmed my conviction that justice was one of my father's chief characteristics. And his sense of justice must have been rooted in a faith in divine justice. Otherwise I cannot imagine how or why he would have formulated the adage that I heard from him so often: "To God's will, I hold still."

My Childhood

Back to my birth. I was born in a dwelling on the top floor of number 6 Czernin Street, in Vienna's second district. If I remember correctly, it was my father who first told me that at number 7, diagonally across the street from us, Dr. Alfred Adler had lived for a time. Thus, the birth of my logotherapy—the "Third Viennese School of Psychotherapy"—took place not far from that of the Second Viennese School, Adler's "individual psychology."

A short walk along Prater Avenue, on the other side of our block, stands the building where the "Blue Danube Waltz" (the unofficial Austrian anthem) was composed by Johann Strauss.

Number 6, Czernin Street, Vienna, Frankl's birthplace.

Logotherapy itself was born in the place of my birth. But the books I have published were all written in the apartment in which we have been living since my return from the concentration camps to Vienna. My study, in which I dictated my books with much "labor pain," I once named the "delivery room."

When I was three, I decided to become a physician, and this probably pleased my father much. The other professions of which we children dreamed at the time—cabin boy on a ship, or officer in the army—I blended in easily by wishing to become a ship's doctor or army doc-

No. 1, Mariannen Street, Vienna, where Frankl has been living since 1945. His work room is the corner room.

tor. But beyond thinking about practice, I must have been interested in research, also at an early age. I remember telling mother when I was four: "I know, Mama, how one invents medicines. One picks out people who want to take their lives anyway, and happen to be sick. You give them all sorts of things to eat and drink—such as shoe polish or gasoline. If they survive, you have discovered the right medicine for their sickness!" And now my critics accuse me of not being research-oriented enough!

Near this same time, one evening just before falling asleep, I was startled by the unexpected thought that one day I too would have to die. What troubled me then—as it has done throughout my life—was not the fear of dying, but the question of whether the transitory nature of life might destroy its meaning. Eventually my struggle brought me to this answer: In some respects it is death itself that makes life meaningful. Most importantly, the transitoriness of life cannot destroy its meaning because nothing from the past is irretrievably lost. Everything is irrevocably stored. It is in the past that things are rescued and preserved from transitoriness. Whatever we have done, or created, whatever we have learned and experienced—all of this we have delivered into the past. There is no one, and nothing, that can undo it.

As a boy I was sorry that, mostly because of World War I, I could not fulfill two desires of my heart. I wanted to become a boy scout and to own a bicycle. On the other hand, I succeeded in something I would not have dared even to hope. Among the hundreds of boys in the city's playgrounds, I wrestled down the one who was acknowledged to be the strongest by getting him into a headlock.

As a very young man I always wanted to write a short story. The plot? Someone is looking feverishly for a lost notebook. Finally it is returned to him, and the finder

Frankl (center) with brother Walter and sister Stella.

wants to know the meaning of the strange entries in the diary pages. They are the key words that remind the writer of his "secret holidays" when something fortunate happened to him. For example, a July 9th entry says, "Railroad station, Brünn." On that day, as a two-year-old, his parents took their eyes off of him for a moment and he climbed out onto the railroad tracks, right in front of a waiting train. Only when the departure whistle blew did his father, who had been searching for him, spot him and dash to pull him away from the tracks—just before the train started moving. Lucky boy, thanks to God, or rather lucky me, since I was myself that little boy.

In my childhood a sense of safety and security seemed natural to me. This came not through philosophical considerations, but through the environment in which I lived. From about the age of five, I have a memory that I consider significant. One sunny morning, during our vacation in Hainfeld, I awakened. With my eyes still closed, I was flooded by the utterly rapturous sense of being guarded, sheltered. When I opened my eyes, my father was standing there, bending over me and smiling.

Now some reflections on my sexual development. I was a little boy when my older brother and I found a packet of pornographic postcards while walking on a family outing in the Vienna Woods. We were neither shocked nor surprised, and we could not understand why mother snatched the photos so quickly from our hands.

Later, perhaps in my eighth year, sex took on an air of secret fascination. The immediate cause was our well-built and bold maid, who presented her body to my brother and me (sometimes separately, sometimes together). She allowed us to remove the clothing from the lower part of her body. By pretending to be asleep on the floor, she encouraged us in this kind of play, even with her genitals. Afterwards, she always warned us strongly never to mention anything to our parents, since this was to be our secret.

For years I became afraid whenever I had done something wrong, even unrelated to sex, because of the way the maid warned me, shaking her forefinger: "Vicky, be good or I'll tell Mama the secret!" Those words were absolutely enough to hold me at bay—until one day I overheard my mother asking the maid: "What exactly is the secret?" The maid answered: "Oh, nothing special. He ate some jam." Her apprehension that I might say something to mother had at least some justification.

I remember clearly that I said to my father one day: "Papa, I did *not* tell you that Marie and I took a ride on the merry-go-round in the Prater yesterday, right?" This was my way of proving that I could keep secrets. Imagine if I had said one day: "Papa, I did *not* tell you that I played with Marie's genitals yesterday, right?"

Eventually I came to understand the relationship between sex and marriage, and this even before I became aware of the connection between sex and propagation. I was probably in junior high school when I decided that, as a married man someday, I would try to stay awake, at least for a while, so I wouldn't miss having sex with my wife while we were "sleeping together." Are people so stupid, I asked myself, that they miss something so beautiful while they are sleeping? I was determined to enjoy it fully awake.

During another family vacation, this time in Pottenstein, a friend of my parents spent a lot of time with us children. She used to call me "The Thinker," probably because I peppered her with questions. I was always asking her about something, wanting to know more and more. In my view I was never a big thinker. But one thing I may have been through my life: a thorough and persistent "thinker-through."

One might call it pondering, or perhaps self-contemplation in the best tradition of Socrates when, during the years of my youth I had breakfast (or just my coffee) in bed, and I would think for some minutes about the meaning of life. Particularly about the meaning of the coming day, and specifically its meaning *for me.*

By this I am reminded of an episode in the Theresienstadt concentration camp. A professor from Prague tested the IQs of some of his colleagues, and mine came out above average. This made me sad because I thought that other people, under different circumstances, would be able to use their intelligence to accomplish something.

The Frankl family, 1925. From left to right: Viktor, Gabriel, Elsa, Stella, and Walter.

But I would probably have no such chance, since I would die in the camp.

Speaking of intelligence, I have always been amused when I heard that others had an idea that I had had a long time before. I didn't mind much because I realized that they had worked hard to publish, while I without effort had had the same idea that gained fame for others through their publications. I suspect that I would not have cared if others had received the Nobel Prize for ideas that had occurred to me also.

The Manner of My Work

As a perfectionist, I tend to ask a great deal of myself. This, of course, does not mean that I always meet my own demands. But whenever I do, I see this as the key to my successes, as far as I have any. When someone asks me how I explain my accomplishments, I usually say: "Because I have made it a principle to give the smallest things the same attention as the biggest, and to do the biggest as calmly as the smallest." Whenever I am asked to make some remarks in a discussion, I think them out and make some notes. In a similar way, when I address as many as several thousand people I always prepare my thoughts meticulously and rely on my notes. Then I try to speak with the same composure as when I comment before a handful of people.

Another thing: I try to do everything as soon as possible, and not at the last moment. This ensures that, when I am overburdened with work, I will not face the added pressure of knowing that something is still to be done. There is yet a third principle that has guided my work, and it is this: I do the unpleasant tasks before I do the pleasant ones. As I have said, I do not always follow my principles. For example, as a young physician I worked in the large Steinhof Mental Hospital and I often spent my Sundays at vaudeville shows. I enjoyed them, but I always regretted that I had not stayed at home to work on my ideas and writing.

Since my years in the concentration camps, this pattern has changed. How many weekends I have sacrificed in order to dictate my books. I have learned to spend my time more wisely, indeed to make every minute count. I do this so that I have time for the things that are really important.

Nevertheless, I must confess that I do not always hold to my principles. But then I am angry with myself— so angry at times that I do not even speak to myself for days.

Emotions and Desires

As stated earlier, I am for the most part a rational person, a man of the mind. At the same time, as I have also said, I am a person of deep feelings as well.

During World War II, even before I was deported to the camps and when euthanasia was being used on the mentally ill, I had a moving dream. Feeling a deep compassion for them, I dreamed that some of these people had been selected and were lined up in front of a gas chamber. After a short deliberation, I joined the people in line. Obvious to me, this dream was triggered by the story of the famous Polish pediatrician, Janusz Korcsak, who had voluntarily followed the children in his care into the gas chamber. He actually did that. I only dreamed it.

Yet I give myself credit for understanding him well. As I have said, I know only a few good qualities in myself, and perhaps only one: I do not forget any good deed done to me, and I carry no grudge for a bad one.

As a student, what did I wish for in my life? I wished for more than I had at the time, namely to have my own automobile and my own house, and to be a lecturer at a university. Eventually I owned a car, but never a house. My third wish has been fulfilled in my role as university professor.

Were there other desires? Yes, and one I can identify exactly. I wanted to make the first ascent of an alpine peak. Once I was invited to do so by my mountain-climbing partner, Rudi Reif. But I could not get the time away from my work at the Steinhof hospital. Incidentally, to me *three* of the most exciting things to do are these: a first ascent, gambling at a casino, and performing brain surgery.

Frankl with his rock-climbing companion Rudi Reif.

It is apparent that I can get over disappointments, thanks perhaps to some insights about living. Often I suggest that others do what I do when facing a setback: I kneel down in my imagination, and pray that nothing worse will happen to me in the future.

What matters is not only what we may be spared in the future, but also what we have been spared in the past. We should be grateful for every good fortune and recall them by establishing days of remembrance. This is what the character in my unwritten short story was doing in his notebook.

When I was very young, perhaps 13 or 14, I planned to write another story. It went like this. A man discovers a medicine that makes a person very smart. The pharmaceutical industry pounces on the news, but cannot find the discoverer. In fact, he had taken the potion himself, and it had made him so smart that he had withdrawn to a primeval forest for contemplation. In other words, he had become so wise that he evaded any commercial exploitation of his secret. I never wrote this story.

I also invented a theory once that I never wrote down either, but I used it to my benefit. During an examination in pathology, Professor Maresch asked me how ulcers develop. I answered him by quoting a certain theory that I remembered from my notes. Then he asked: "Good, but there are other theories. Do you know any?"

I answered, "Yes, of course," and I described another theory.

"And who developed it?" he wanted to know.

I stuttered in embarrassment until he helped me out by mentioning a famous name. "Of course," I said. "How could I forget that?"

Actually, I had invented the theory on the spot.

On Wit and Humor

Punning and other forms of humor have been among my pleasures. Sometimes they result in word monstrosities, but that doesn't stop me.

Many times I am offered a second cup of tea. I decline it by saying, "No thanks. I am a mono-tea-ist. I only drink *one* cup."

For much of my life I neither owned nor drove an automobile. So I would tell people: "You know, I usually travel in a heteromobile, that is, in somebody else's car."

Everyone knows how humor can enliven a lecture, and even make it harder for an opponent to argue during discussion. In my opening lecture at the "Styrian Autumn"[6] festival in Graz, I wanted to indicate that I was qualified to speak both as a medical man and as a philosopher, yet I wanted to play down the fact that I had a doctorate in each field. So I said: "Ladies and gentlemen, I have both medical and philosophy doctorates, but usually I do not mention this. Knowing my dear colleagues in Vienna, I expect that instead of saying Frankl is twice a doctor, they would say he is only half a physician."

During audience questions following a lecture in Munich, a young man challenged me: "*Herr Frankl*, you are talking about sex. But how can a busy professor have time for a healthy sex life, or even know much about it?"

"You know, my friend," I replied, "your words remind me of an old Viennese joke. A man greets a baker and hears that he has ten children. He asks him, 'Tell me, when do you have time to bake?'" The audience laughed.

I continued: "That is what you remind me of: you doubt that someone, who during the day has academic duties, can at night lead a normal sex life." Now the laughter was on my side.

During another question period I was not about to embarrass someone else, and wanted to spare myself as well. In the theological school of an American university, I was asked after a lecture what I thought of theologian Paul Tillich's[7] concept of "the God above God." I had never heard of the concept, but answered calmly: "If I answer your question regarding 'the God above God' it would imply that I consider myself a Tillich above Tillich."

I love jokes, and I love to make jokes. For a long while I toyed with the idea of writing a book on the metaphysical background of jokes. A favorite of mine is about the stranger who arrives in a Polish village with a large Jewish population. He is looking for a brothel. Embarrassed to ask directly, he stops an old Jew in a caftan on the street and asks him: "Where does the rabbi live?" The answer is: "Over there, in that house painted green."

"What?" shouts the stranger, pretending to be shocked. "Such a famous rabbi, and he lives in a brothel?"

"How can you say such a thing?" is the Jew's reproach. "The brothel is that red house, over there."

Such an indirect approach is often used by physicians with their patients. As a young doctor I learned that, when taking down the medical history of a new female patient, one must not ask: "Have you ever had an abortion?" Rather ask, "*How often* have you had abortions?"

Or, the doctor must never ask a man: "Did you ever have syphilis?" Rather: "*How many* Salvarsan treatments have you had?"

Neither is it advisable to ask a person with schizophrenia whether he hears voices, but rather: "What are the voices telling you?"

Psychosomatic medicine takes a blow in the following joke. A man is sent to a psychoanalyst because he suffers from headaches, congestion in the head, and ringing in the ears—and the analyst will undoubtedly find many deep, unconscious causes for these symptoms. On his way to the appointment, however, the man passes a clothing store and remembers that he needs a new shirt. He enters and asks for a certain brand.

"What size?" asks the sales clerk.

"Fifteen" is the answer.

"I'm sure you need at least a 16."

"Give me a 15 and no questions."

"Okay, but don't be surprised if you suffer from headaches, congestion in the head, and ringing in the ears."

The effects of ingested substances lead us to a joke that may enlighten us on pharmacopsychiatry. This one is from the Nazi era. An SS man shares a train compartment with a Jew. The Jew unpacks a herring, eats it, then wraps the head carefully and puts it in his pocket. The SS man asks why he is doing this.

"The head of the fish contains the brain. I bring it home to my children, so that they'll become smart."

"How much will you take for the head?" asks the guard.

"One mark."

"Here is your mark," says the SS man, and he eats the fish head. Five minutes later he goes into a rage. "You dirty cheat! The whole fish costs only half a mark, and you charged me a mark just for the head!"

"See?" said the Jew. "It's beginning to work already."

There is a difference between treating causes and treating symptoms, and a joke may help to explain it. During a vacation in the country, a man is awakened early every morning by a crowing rooster. So the vacationer goes to a pharmacy, buys sleeping pills, and mixes them with the rooster's feed. This is the treatment of causes.

There may be more than one explanation for drug dependence, and sometimes I have illustrated it with this story. An alcoholic comes to his doctor because his hearing is impaired, and the doctor tells him to stop drinking. After a month they meet, and the doctor asks: "How are you doing?"

"No need to shout, doctor. I followed your advice and my hearing is much improved."

Another month goes by, and the man meets his doctor once again. But this time the man is stone deaf. The doctor asks him what happened. The man answers: "You know, Doc, at first I drank and heard poorly. Then I stopped drinking and heard much better. But *what* I heard was not nearly as good as the whiskey."

Example is more powerful than talk, as modern psychological research on "modeling" has shown us. The following joke illuminates this. A man buys himself a parrot. He wants his bird to call him "Uncle" and proceeds to train it, using brutal methods that are not successful. He finally resorts to a new punishment: He locks the parrot in the henhouse with the chickens for the night. In the morning, the man goes into the henhouse and finds the parrot attacking the last surviving hen. The parrot is screeching repeatedly: "Say 'uncle' to me, say 'uncle' to me . . ."

Pleasures and Hobbies

When reflecting on character traits and personality, and how they find expression, we should also mention pleasures and hobbies. Therefore, I confess the importance of coffee to me. On every lecture tour I carry a caffeine tablet for the emergency when no strong coffee is available. One day, in the Austrian town of Gmunden, I ordered a cappuccino—a strong coffee as brown as the robe of a Capuchin monk. But the waiter brought me what we call in Vienna "dishwater"—a weak, thin cup of coffee. I rushed back to the hotel to get my tablet, and who stops me in the lobby? A real, live Capuchin monk! He had brought a few of my books from the cloister library for me to autograph.

Until my 80th year, mountain climbing was my most passionate hobby. When I was not permitted to go to the Alps because I am a Jew and had to wear the yellow star, I *dreamed* about climbing. One time my friend, Hubert Gsur, persuaded me, and I dared to go to the mountains *without* my Jewish star. I literally kissed the rock.

Climbing is the only sport of which one can say that the diminishing strength due to aging can be compensated by greater climbing experience and techniques. In any case, my hours spent in climbing were the only ones during which I gave no thought to my next lecture or book. And it was not an exaggeration when Juan Battista Torello[8] wrote in an Austrian school newspaper of his suspicion that all my honorary doctorates do not mean as much to me as the three Alpine climbing paths named in my honor by those who first conquered them (now called "Frankl-climbs").

Remember my mention of three exciting things (brain surgery, a roulette game, and a first ascent)? To them I must add the happy moments after completing a book and taking the manuscript to the publisher in the city; then to go to the mountains, climb a sheer rock wall, and spend the night in a mountain lodge with a loved one. I go to the mountains as some go to the desert: to gather my strength on solitary walks, as on the plateau of the Rax Mountain.[9] Every important decision I have made, almost without exception, I have made in the mountains.

I have climbed not only the Alps, but also the High Tatra Mountains in the former Czechoslovakia. There my wife, Elly, and I have climbed a most difficult ridge. On the occasion of an anniversary lectureship at the University of Stellenbosch, we climbed Table Mountain in Cape Town, South Africa. Our guide then was the president of the South African Mountain Climbing Club. By coincidence, my wife and I were the first students of the newly opened climbing school in Yosemite National Park, California.

Some of my friends suspect that my passion for mountain climbing is related to my interest in "height

Frankl on a climbing tour in the Tyrol (1948).

psychology," as I have called logotherapy, which I first identified as such in a 1938 publication. This is in contrast to the depth psychologies, which delve into the dark mysteries of unconscious dynamics. The suspicion of my friends is further supported by another "reaching for the heights" when, at age 67, I took my first flying lessons during my professorship in San Diego, California. This city is on the Pacific Coast, where there are no mountains to climb. After a few months I took my first solo flights.

May I mention also some less serious interests? One of these is neckties. I can even fall in love with ties, in a "Platonic" sense. By this I mean that I can admire them in a shop window, knowing that they are not mine and that I shall never own them.

Frankl as pilot in California.

A hobby can almost develop into a profession. I am very knowledgeable with regard to the design of eyeglass frames. One of the world's largest manufacturers considered my knowledge professional enough to consult with me on sketches of their designs before beginning production.

I have not hesitated to dabble with other things as well. I have composed music, including the score of an elegy that was arranged by a professional musician and performed by an orchestra. A tango I wrote was used in a television program.

Incidentally, some decades ago I was invited by the head of a mental hospital to give several days of symposia on logotherapy. This was in Vickersund, Norway, an hour's drive from Oslo.

"Is someone going to introduce me at my first lecture?" I asked.

"Yes," he said.

"And who will it be?"

"The new full professor of psychiatry at the University of Oslo."

"Does he know anything about me?"

"Not only does he know you, but he told me he has held you in high esteem for years."

I could not recall the man, and I was curious. When he appeared, he assured me that he had known me for a long time. It turned out that he was one of the children of the *Schammes*, the keeper of the synagogue in Pohorlice in southern Moravia, the birthplace of my father.

Our family spent summer vacations there during the worst starvation period of World War I. My older brother was very good at organizing amateur theater performances. They took place in the yards of farmhouses, where the stages were wooden planks supported by barrels. The ensemble was composed of 13 to 15-year-old boys and girls. I was among them. I play old Dr. Stieglitz with a bald-headed wig, and the drunken cobbler Knieriem in the popular farce *Lumpazivagabundus,* by Johann Nestroy. The man who introduced me at the lecture was Professor Eitinger, a well-known professor of psychiatry at Oslo, who must have been a small boy at the time of our dramatic performances, since he is a few years younger than I. After all these years, he had hardly heard of logotherapy but never forgot Viktor Frankl's drunken Knieriem.

In the preface of the latest edition of my book, *...trotzdem Ja zum Leben sagen*[10] [*Say Yes to Life in Spite of Everything*], it is mentioned that I once wrote a play. (It is interesting that the book itself has been dramatized by a Catholic priest in Australia.) One act of the drama was performed in the largest hall in Toronto as a prelude to my lecture there. "Viktor Frankl" appears in the play twice: once as inmate of the camp, and again as commentator. I was the "third" Viktor Frankl, actually seated in that theater.

School Days

During World War I, civil servants had a very tough time financially. We no longer could afford our summer vacation spots, but went to Pohorlice, father's birthplace. We children went to local farmers to beg bread, or we stole corn from the fields.

In Vienna I stood in lines from 3 a.m. just to buy some potatoes; mother came to take my place at 7:30 so I could go to school. And this was in winter.

Then came the hectic time between the great wars. Meanwhile I had started to read eagerly the books by natural philosophers such as Wilhelm Ostwald[11] and Gustav Theodor Fechner.[12] I had not yet come across Fechner's work when I had filled several notebooks and chose the ambitious title, "We and the Workings of the World." I was already becoming persuaded of some kind of balancing principle at work in the universe.

Once, when we were traveling upstream on a Danube River boat to a vacation spot (Eferding), I was lying on the deck around midnight. I glanced up at the starry sky above and thought of the principle within (to paraphrase Kant). I had the "aha experience" that nirvana is much like the "heat death" of physical cosmology, "seen from within." I was convinced that there is some kind of universal homeostatic principle, that there is an overall trend in the universe toward some kind of "rest state" or equilibrium.

It is clear that Fechner later made an impression on me with his "day versus night views," and still later I became fascinated with Sigmund Freud's "Beyond the Pleasure Principle." This brings us to my confrontation with psychoanalysis.

Until junior high I was on the school honor rolls, but then I began to follow my own interests. I attended adult evening classes on applied psychology and I also became interested in experimental psychology. When giving reports in school, I would use activities with my lectures, one of which was Veraguth's psychogalvanic reflex phenomenon. A classmate had to "volunteer." After a few words, I spoke the name of his girlfriend and the pointer on the galvanometer, projected on the laboratory wall, jumped across its range. At the time one still was embarrassed on such occasions but, fortunately for my classmate, the classroom was too dark to see him blush.

Arguments with Psychoanalysis

More and more my speech and writing assignments became treatises on psychoanalysis. Increasingly I was providing information to my schoolmates about it. Everyone knew what went on in the unconscious of our logic professor when he produced a Freudian slip by talking, not about the population of Vienna, but about its *copulation*.

My first knowledge was gathered from Freud's own influential students such as Eduard Hirschmann[13] and Paul Schilder,[14] who regularly gave lectures in the University Psychiatric Clinic of Wagner von Jauregg.[15]

Before long I was corresponding with Freud. I sent him material that I came across in my interdisciplinary readings and that I thought would interest him. He promptly answered every letter.

Unfortunately, all of Freud's letters and postcards—our entire correspondence through my high school years—were confiscated by the Gestapo years later when I was deported to the concentration camps. Also taken from me were a few case histories the young Freud had written by hand during his time at the university's psychiatric clinic. These had been given to me by the keeper of the archives when I worked there.

One day I sat on a bench in the Prater Park—my favorite working place at the time—and put down on paper whatever came to my mind regarding "the origin of the mimic movements of affirmation and negation." I enclosed the manuscript in a letter to Freud. I was more than surprised when Freud wrote to me that he had sent my article on to the *International Journal of Psychoanalysis*, hoping I would not object.

Eduard Hirschmann (top) and Paul Schilder.

Sigmund Freud.

And indeed, later on, in 1924, it was published in that journal. My first publication, however, had appeared in 1923 in the youth supplement of a daily paper. It is rather ironic that this article by a psychiatrist-to-be started with the statement that he hated nothing more than common sense. (I was attempting to criticize the blind acceptance of merely traditional thoughts.)

Those who know me also know that my opposition to Freud's ideas never kept me from showing him the respect he deserves. Perhaps my respect is illustrated by a suggestion I made when I was vice president of the Austrian Society in Support of the Hebrew University in Jerusalem: that a campus building there, for which we were seeking funds, be named "Sigmund Freud Hall."

Not only did I correspond with Freud, but I met him once by chance while I was a university student. When I introduced myself he asked immediately: "Viktor Frankl—Vienna second district, Czerningasse 6, door 25, right?"

"Correct," I nodded. Apparently he knew my address by heart from our long exchange of letters and cards.

If that meeting was by chance, it was also too late. By that time I had come under the influence of Alfred Adler, who had accepted my second scientific paper for the *International Journal of Individual Psychology* in 1925. The impression Freud made on me, so different from that of Adler, is beyond the scope of this little book to describe. Kurt Eissler,[16] head of the Freud archive in New York, asked me on one of his visits to Vienna if I would write down in detail my recollection of my encounter with Freud and to make an audiotape of it. This I did, and it was added to the archive.

Psychiatry as My Chosen Profession

I was still in high school when the wish of my early childhood to be a physician became more focused and, under the influence of psychoanalysis, I became interested in psychiatry.

For a while I had toyed with the idea of specializing in dermatology or obstetrics. One day, another medical student, W. Oesterreicher, who later settled in Amsterdam, asked me if I had ever heard of Søren Kierkegaard. Somehow my interests in fields other than psychiatry had reminded him of Kierkegaard's line: "Don't despair at

The three schools of Viennese psychotherapy: (1) Sigmund Freud;
(2) Alfred Adler; (3) Viktor Frankl.

wanting to become your authentic self." This student told me that I was gifted for psychiatry and that I should own up to my talent.

It is difficult to believe what decisive turns in our lives we sometimes owe to even casual remarks made by another person. In any case, from that moment on I made up my mind that I would no longer avoid my "psychiatric self-actualization."

But then I asked myself: Am I really gifted for psychiatry? If this is so, it might be related to another of my talents: my gift as a cartoonist.

As a cartoonist, just as a psychiatrist, I can spot the weaknesses in a person. But as a psychiatrist, or rather a psychotherapist, I can see beyond the actual weaknesses and can also recognize intuitively some possibilities for overcoming those weaknesses. I can see beyond the misery of the situation to the potential for discovering a meaning behind it, and thus to turn *an apparently meaningless suffering into a genuine human achievement*. I am convinced that, in the final analysis, there is no situation that does not contain within it the seed of a meaning. To a great extent, this conviction is the basis of logotherapy.

But what is the use of having a talent for psychiatry without the urge to become a psychiatrist? We must ask ourselves not only what enables a person in this profession, but what motivates him or her? I believe that for immature people the lure of psychiatry lies in its promise to *gain power over others*, to dominate and manipulate them. Knowledge is power, and so knowledge of some mechanisms possessed by us and not by others gives us power over them.

This is most obvious in the case of hypnosis. I admit to an early interest in hypnosis and, at age 15, was able to use it correctly.

In my book *Psychotherapie für den Alltag* [*Psychotherapy In Everyday Life*] I describe how, as an intern in the department of gynecology at Vienna's Rothschild Hospital, I had to perform a narcosis in preparation for a surgery. My supervisor and head of the department, Dr. Fleischmann, gave me the honorable but not very promising order to hypnotize a small, old woman who could not take a regular narcotic for her surgery. For some reason, a local anesthetic was also not possible. Thus I tried to keep the poor woman pain-free through hypnosis. The attempt was successful.

But an unexpected surprise awaited me. For, mixed in with the praises from the physicians and the thanks of the patient were the most bitter and vehement reproaches by the nurse who had handled the surgical instruments during the operation. She let me know with her rebuke that she had had to use every bit of her willpower to fight off sleepiness during the entire procedure. My monotone suggestions had had their effect not only on the patient.

Another time, as a young doctor in the Maria Theresien Schlössel Neurological Hospital, I experienced the following. My supervisor, Dr. Josef Gerstmann,[17] had asked me to induce sleep in a patient who suffered from insomnia and was staying in a two-bed room. Late in the evening I quietly stole into the room, sat near his bed, and repeated for at least half an hour the hypnotic suggestions: "You are calm, very calm, pleasantly tired. You are getting more and more tired. Your breathing is calm, your eyelids are becoming heavier and heavier. All your worries are far, far away. Soon you'll fall asleep."

But when I tried to slip out of the room quietly, I was disappointed to see that I had not helped the man. How surprised I was, however, at the enthusiastic welcome when I entered the same patient room the next day. "I slept wonderfully last night. A few minutes after you started talking I was in a deep sleep." But this was the *roommate* of the man I had been sent to hypnotize.

The Influence of the Physician

Power, schmower. I agree with John Ruskin,[18] who once said: "There is only one power: the power to save someone. And there is only one honor: the honor to help someone." It must have been 1930 when I gave a course in a Vienna adult education program on mental illnesses, their causes, and prevention (note: *not* their diagnosis and treatment). I remember how I entered the classroom at dusk, and the electric lights were not yet on. I explained to an attentive audience of a few dozen people the significance of a meaning orientation, and that life has meaning, unconditionally. I felt strongly that these people were receptive to my words and that I had succeeded in giving them something worthwhile—even that they had, in a sense, been "clay in the potter's hand." In this way, perhaps, I had made use of my "power to save."

As the Talmud says: "He who saves but one soul is to be regarded as one who has saved the whole world."

I also remember the not-so-young daughter of a world-famous zoologist who had been my patient in a mental hospital in 1930. She suffered from a severe obsessive–compulsive neurosis and had been a patient for many years. Again it was dusk, and I sat on the edge of the empty bed next to hers and spoke to her persuasively. I did my best to motivate her to distance herself from her compulsive actions. I responded to all her arguments and countered all her fears. She became calmer and calmer, less and less burdened, less and less depressed. Clearly, every one of my words fell on fertile ground. And again I had the experience of "clay in the potter's hand."

Philosophical Questions

As a youth I remained enthusiastic about psychiatry, and about psychoanalysis particularly. I was also fascinated by philosophy. The adult education school offered a philosophical workshop led by Edgar Zilsel. When I was 15 or 16 I gave a lecture there; the subject was "The Meaning of Life." Even at that early age I had developed two basic ideas. First, it is not we who should ask for the meaning of life, since it is we who *are being asked*. It is we ourselves who must answer the questions that life asks of us, and to these questions we can respond only by being responsible for our existence.

The other basic idea I developed in my early years maintains that ultimate meaning is, and must remain, beyond our comprehension. There exists something I have called "suprameaning," *but not in the sense of something supernatural*. In this we can only believe. In this we must believe. Even if only unconsciously, essentially we all do believe in it.

It must have been at that time, at the same age, that one Sunday I was on one of my typical walks through the streets of Vienna. At a certain spot on Tabor Street, I pondered what I almost might call a hymn-like thought: *Blessed be fate, believed be meaning.*

By this I meant that, whatever we have to go through, life must have ultimate meaning, a suprameaning. This suprameaning we cannot comprehend, we can only have faith in it. In the last analysis this was only a rediscovery of Spinoza's *amor fati*—the love of fate.

Faith

As for faith, I have written and talked about it a great deal. I have devoted a substantial part of my literary work to the mutual boundaries between psychotherapy and theology or, as Fritz Künkel[19] phrased it, the difference between the healing of the soul and the salvation of the soul.

First of all, it depends in what manner I speak of faith—as psychiatrist, philosopher, physician, or simply as a human being. Second, I went through various developmental stages: As a child I was religious, but then, during puberty, I passed through an atheistic period.

And third, we need to consider the audience to whom we speak. I would not dream of confessing my personal faith when speaking about logotherapeutic methods and techniques to psychiatrists. This would not serve the spreading of logotherapeutic ideas, which, after all, is my responsibility.

In my more recent publications I often discuss the question of what we call "pure coincidence," and whether behind an apparent coincidence a higher, or deeper, ultimate meaning may be hidden.

This reminds me of the following episode. One day I passed Vienna's Votiv Church (which I have always loved because it is "pure Gothic," though its construction was begun in 1856). I had never been inside. But my wife and I heard organ music, and I suggested to her that we go in and sit down for awhile.

As soon as we entered, the music stopped and the priest stepped to the pulpit and began to preach. And he began to speak of the nearby Berggasse 19 and of the "godless" Sigmund Freud who had lived there. Then he continued: "But we don't need to go so far, not to Berg-

Votiv Church in Vienna.

gasse. Right behind us, at Mariannengasse 1, lives a Viktor Frankl who wrote a book, *Die ärztliche Seelsorge* [literally, "the medical ministry," with the English edition title, *The Doctor and the Soul*]—a godless book indeed." The priest proceeded to tear my book to shreds. Later I introduced myself, a bit worried that this encounter might give him a heart attack. He certainly had not expected that I would be present. How many minutes had passed from my birth up to that sermon, up to the point of our visit to the Votiv Church for the first time? How minuscule is the chance that I would enter at exactly the moment when the priest mentioned me in his sermon?

I think the only appropriate attitude to such coincidences is to not even try to explain them. Anyway, I am too ignorant to explain them, and too smart to deny them.

Back to my 15th or 16th year. As I have said, I began to philosophize. But I was still too immature to resist the temptation of psychologism. Even later on, in my high school paper that I entitled "The Psychology of Philosophical Thinking," I still advanced a psychoanalytically oriented pathology of Arthur Schopenhauer—but at least I had let go of the notion that what is sick must be wrong. As I stated it later in *The Doctor and the Soul:* "Two and two make four, even if a schizophrenic says it."

To the temptation of psychologism was added that of sociologism. While I was in high school I was, for years, a functionary of the Social Democratic youth movement. And during part of 1924 I was the managing president of the movement for socialist high school students throughout Austria. My friends and I roamed through the Prater Park half through the night, discussing the alternatives of Marx or Lenin, and also of Freud and Adler.

What had been the theme of my article that Adler published in his journal? The theme runs like a radiant thread through all my work, and it concerns *the border area that lies between psychotherapy and philosophy, with special attention to the problems of meanings and values in psychology.* And I must say, I hardly know anyone who has wrestled with that problem as long as I have.

It is the leitmotif behind all my work. The primary motivation to do this work, however, has been my effort to overcome the psychologism in the field of psychotherapy where it usually coexists with a "pathologism." But both are aspects of a more comprehensive phenomenon, namely reductionism, which also includes sociologism and biologism. Reductionism is today's nihilism. It reduces a human being, by no less than an entire dimension, namely the specific human dimension. It projects what is uniquely human from the three-dimensional domain of the total human being into the two-dimensional plane of the subhuman. In other words, reductionism is subhumanism.

Encounter with Individual Psychology

Now let us return to Adler. In 1925 my article "Psychotherapy and World View" was published in his *Journal of Individual Psychology*. In 1926 another one followed. The same year I was asked to give the keynote address at the International Congress for Individual Psychology in Düsseldorf, but I could not do so without deviating from the orthodox line of the congress. I denied that every neurosis, always and everywhere, is a mere means to an end in the sense of the doctrine of its "arrangement character." I insisted upon the alternative to see it not as a mere "means," but also as a symptom, which means not only in an instrumental, but also in an expressive, sense.

On this, my first lecture tour, I stopped off to address audiences in Frankfurt and Berlin. In Frankfurt—it is hard to believe and almost laughable—I, a medical student of 21 years, lectured on the meaning of life at the invitation of the Young Socialist Workers. Entire columns of young people, carrying flags, marched from a gathering place to my lecture. At Berlin I lectured for the Society for Individual Psychology.

In 1927 my relationship with Adler deteriorated. I had come under the spell of two men who impressed me

Alfred Adler (1934).

not only as persons, but who also had a lasting influence on me through their ideas: Rudolf Allers and Oswald Schwarz.[20] I began to work under Allers at his Laboratory of the Physiology of the Senses. Schwarz, founder of psychosomatic medicine and a medical anthropologist, did me the honor of supplying the foreword for a book I was asked to write for the Hirzel publishing house. It never saw the light of day because, in the meantime, I was expelled from the Society for Individual Psychology. This "departure" I shall describe in more detail. (A short version of the central ideas of that "aborted" book appeared in 1939 in the *Schweizerische medizinische Wochenschrift* the

[*Swiss Medical Weekly*]). In his foreword, Schwarz stated that my book meant for the history of psychotherapy what Kant's "Critique of Pure Reason" meant for philosophy.

At that time I finally saw through my own psychologism. My ultimate shakeup came from Max Scheler[21] whose *Formalismus in der Ethik* [*Formalism in Ethics*] I carried with me like a bible. It was the highest time for such self-criticism. I had already been invited, by the wise bohemian among the Adlerians, Alexander Neuer, to join in a conversation in the literary café in Vienna, the "Herrenhof." First he told me that, on the basis of my writings that he had read, he had concluded that I had priority over Max Planck's attempt to resolve the problem of freedom of the will, and also over Gestalt psychology. But then he started, again on the basis of my writings, to upbraid me passionately as a "renegade of the spirit." That hurt. But from that time forward I was no longer as willing to compromise.

Then came the evening in 1927 when Allers and Schwarz were openly to announce and to justify their withdrawal from the Society for Individual Psychology, a decision that they had earlier made known privately. The session took place in the large lecture hall of the Histological Institute of the University of Vienna. In the back rows sat a few Freudians, who enjoyed the spectacle of watching Adler experience the same fate that Freud himself met when Adler withdrew from the Society for Psychoanalysis. Here again was a "secession." The presence of psychoanalysts made Adler all the more sensitive.

When Allers and Schwarz had concluded their remarks, there was a heavy tension in the air. How would Adler react? We waited in vain. Embarrassing minutes passed. I was seated near Adler in the first row. Between us sat one of his students, whose reservations about Adler's ideas were as well known to Adler as my own reservations. Finally, Adler turned to us and scoffed, "Well, you heroes?" What he wanted to say was that we should have the courage to show our true colors by speaking up.

So I had no choice but to step up in front of everyone present and to explain how individual psychology still had to free itself from psychologism. And I made the mistake of declaring myself, right in front of the "enemy" psychoanalysts, in favor of Schwarz and even called him "my teacher." It was not much help that I asserted that I saw no reason to leave the Society for Individual Psychology because I believed that we members could overcome our psychologism. In vain I tried to build bridges between Allers, Schwarz, and Adler.

From that evening on, Adler never spoke a word to me again, never acknowledged my greetings when, on many evenings, I approached his table in the Café Siller where he held court. He could not get over the fact that I had not supported him unconditionally.

Repeatedly he had others suggest to me that I should resign from the society, but still I saw no reason for that. A few months later I was expelled formally.

This exodus was significant for me. For one year I had been editor of a journal of individual psychology, *Der Mensch im Alltag* [*The Person in Daily Living*]. In this and in other ways I lost my forum. Few individual psychologists stood with me as scientists or as persons. In relation to this, I gratefully remember Erwin Wexberg,[22] who died when he was very young; Rudolf Dreikurs[23]; and last, but not least, Adler's own daughter, Alexandra. Sometimes I am told that logotherapy is simply "Adlerian psychology at its best" and that there is no reason to regard it as a distinct school of thought or to give it its own name. My response is typically this: Who is best qualified to decide that logotherapy is still individual psychology, or that it is not—who more than Adler himself? It was he who insisted that I be expelled from the society. *Roma locuta causa finita.*

The Beginnings of Logotherapy

Meanwhile, Fritz Wittels,[24] the first Freud biographer, Maximilian Silbermann, and I had founded the Academic Society for Medical Psychology, and I was elected its vice-president. Silbermann was president, and his successors were Fritz Redlich[25] and Peter Hofstätter.[26] On the advisory board were Freud, Schilder,[14] and the notables of Vienna in the 1920s, then the Mecca of psychotherapy. It was in the study group of this society that I gave a lecture before an academic audience and first spoke of logotherapy. The alternative term, *Existenzanalyse (existential analysis)*, I used from 1933 on. By that time I had systematized my ideas to some extent.

As early as 1929 I had developed the concept of three groups of values, or three possible ways to find meaning in life—even up to the last moment, the last breath. The three possibilities are: 1) a deed we do, a work we create; 2) an experience, a human encounter, a love; and 3) when confronted with an unchangeable fate (such as an incurable disease), a change of attitude toward that fate. In such cases we still can wrest meaning from life by giving testimony to the most human of all human capacities: the ability to turn suffering into a human triumph.

It was Wolfgang Soucek who dubbed logotherapy "the Third Viennese School of Psychotherapy." One

Frankl as a medical student (1929).

could say that Haeckel's basic biogenetic law was confirmed in me—the law that says ontogenesis repeats phylogenesis in abbreviated form—for, somehow, I personally had passed through the first two schools of Vienna's psychotherapy, also in abbreviated form, since in 1924 (as already noted) one of my articles had been published on recommendation of Freud, and only a year later another appeared in Adler's journal at his own recommendation.

So I participated in the development of psychotherapy, but I also anticipated some developments. I will only mention paradoxical intention, which I began to use in 1929 and named only later, in 1939 in the *Schweizer Archiv für Neurologie und Psychiatrie* [*Swiss Archive for Neurology and Psychiatry*]. Since then, distinguished behavior therapists often have pointed out that paradoxical intention anticipated behavioral treatment methods developed in the 1960s. Also, in my 1947 book *Die Psychotherapy in der Praxis* [*Psychotherapy in Practice*], I described in detail treatments for impotence which, in the '70s, were hailed as a "new sex therapy" by Masters and Johnson.[27]

I am indebted to behavior therapy in many ways. It pulled, as it were, the chestnuts out of the fire for me in my struggle against psychoanalysis and against individual psychology. To apply a German proverb: When these two schools fight with each other, the third (Viennese school) rejoices. I am always glad if logotherapy does not have to criticize others, even when criticism is fully justified and long overdue.

As for logotherapy itself, it was no less an authority than Gordon Allport[28] of Harvard, in his foreword to *Man's Search for Meaning*, who called it "the most significant psychological movement of our day." And Juan Battista Torello[8] said that it presented the last true system in the history of psychotherapy. If this is so, then Szondi's[29] fate analysis should be mentioned as another highly systematized theory; however, the systematizing is the only, and purely formal, similarity between our contributions. Personally, I consider the Szondi test a fine play with ideas, but nothing more.

Torello claims that I would take my place in the history of psychiatry as the man who therapeutically tackled the sickness of the century, the sense of meaninglessness.

It is true that logotherapy, when all is said and done, was developed for that purpose.

But if one searches for the ultimate causes and deepest roots, the hidden reasons for my creating logotherapy, I can only name one thing that spurred me on to develop and to continue working on logotherapy tirelessly: the compassion I feel toward the victims of today's cynicism, which has also infested psychotherapy, that rotten trade. When I say "trade" I refer to its commercialism, and by "rotten" I mean its scientific uncleanness. If one faces patients who not only suffer psychologically, but who in addition have been harmed by psychotherapy, one's heart goes out to them. And indeed, the fight against these depersonalizing and dehumanizing tendencies, which have their roots in the psychologism of psychotherapy, has been a bright red thread that runs throughout the fabric of my work.

We logotherapists have developed a few techniques. Paradoxical intention is well known, but less so is the technique of the common denominator. This reminds me that Ilse Aichinger,[30] today a well-known writer, came to me when she was still a medical student. She was in a dilemma, having to decide whether to continue writing the novel she had started (the one that made her famous) or to remain in her medical studies. After a long talk, she decided that it was less of a problem to interrupt her studies temporarily than to postpone the completion of the novel. The common denominator was the question: Which is more at risk if interrupted?

As to paradoxical intention, I recall once using it to get out of a traffic ticket. I had driven through a yellow light. The policeman who had pulled me over approached me menacingly. I greeted him with a flood of self-accusations: "You're right, officer. How could I do such a thing? I have no excuse. I am sure I will never do it again, and this will be a lesson to me. This is certainly a crime that deserves punishment."

The officer did his best to calm and reassure me by telling me not to worry—that such a thing could happen to anyone, that he was sure I would never do it again.

Let's return to my years of psychiatric apprenticeship and, more specifically, to my activities as I drifted away from the Society for Individual Psychology.

Theory and Practice: Youth Counseling Centers

After my expulsion from the Adlerian society, the focus of my interests shifted from theory to practice. I organized youth counseling centers, first in Vienna, and then in six other cities, based on the Vienna model. To these centers young people in personal and psychological distress could turn for counseling. Such persons as August Aichhorn,[31] Erwin Wexberg,[22] and Rudolf Dreikurs[23] volunteered as counselors without remuneration. Charlotte Bühler[32] also made herself available to assist counselees and pioneered with a special project for students when the greatly feared high school report cards were issued. That was the first in many years when no student suicides were reported in Vienna.

Other countries began to show interest in this work, and I was invited to give lectures on the subject. In Berlin I had an extensive talk with Wilhelm Reich,[33] who showed an interest in youth counseling. To discuss my experiences with pertinent sexual problems, he drove me around for hours in an open convertible through the

Charlotte Bühler.

streets of Berlin. In Prague and Budapest I gave lectures at the universities. In Prague I met Otto Pötzl,[34] who later became the successor to Wagner von Jauregg[15] in Vienna. Pötzl became, and remained, my lifelong, fatherly friend.

Beside Freud and Adler, Pötzl was for me the personification of genius—and absent-minded as geniuses usually are. The following story is true as I now tell it. One day he came to me in the Policlinic where, as you may remember, I was head of neurology. I led him to my office, and he put his umbrella in the stand. When we parted, he said goodbye and I led him to the door. After a while he returned, since he had forgotten his umbrella.

Otto Pötzl (head of the Department of Neurology and Psychiatry of the University Clinic, Vienna from 1928 to 1945).

He took it and left again. Then I noticed that he had taken my umbrella by mistake, so I called out after him: *"Herr Professor, you have my umbrella!"*

"Excuse me," he said, and took his umbrella. When he had left I saw that he had not returned my umbrella. Again, I ran after him and said, "Excuse me, *Herr Professor*, but this time you have taken both umbrellas."

He apologized again, and came back the third time to return mine. Finally, he took *his* umbrella and *no other!*

At the invitation of Margaret Roller, of the German Youth Welfare Service, I gave a lecture in Brünn; afterward we went together for dinner. She suddenly became pensive. She remembered that for several years she had worked with my father for the Youth Welfare Service and now, here she was working with his son.

(This was true: My father had founded, together with Minister Josef Maria von Bärnreither,[5] the Center for Child Protection and Youth Welfare. In my younger years I could think of nothing more boring than welfare—that is until Margaret Roller made me see that I, too, in my work in youth counseling, was serving the youth welfare movement, although through the field of psychology.)

I had to leave the restaurant and Margaret Roller in a rush to fly to Vienna—in 1930!—as the only passenger in a four-passenger machine. How much of a "load" I was had been ascertained on a scale at the airport. At that time the pilot still sat out in the open, not in a cabin. The flight was my first, and for me it was an adventure. But without the flight it would have been impossible to reach Vienna in time for the class I was teaching. It was, incidentally, the first course in psychological hygiene ever offered by the adult education school.

This reminds me that whenever I wanted to impress a girl, which I could not do with my looks alone, I used a little trick. Assume that I met her at a dance. I would praise a certain Frankl whose class I was attending at the adult school, and I would enthusiastically suggest that she accompany me to hear him speak. And so we would sit down in the big hall on Zirkus Street where this Frankl taught his popular classes. With wise foresight I would sit at the end of the first row. One can imagine the impression it would make on the girl as her date suddenly left his seat and, greeted with audience applause, step up to the lectern.

I also offered lectures for organizations of the socialist youth movement. Through these hundreds of lectures, with their subsequent discussion periods, I gained a trea-

Frankl's first press photo in front of the clinic Am Rosenhügel in Vienna, on occasion of a program he initiated: counseling high school students before the dreaded final exam (1930).

sure chest of experience. This was added to all I had learned from the thousands of young people who came to our counseling centers.

Perhaps it was this experience that prompted Professor Pötzl, for the first and apparently the only time, to make an exception and give permission to Otto Kogerer, chief of psychotherapy at Pötzl's clinic, to let me work there as a psychotherapist without supervision even before my graduation from medical school. I tried to forget what I had learned from psychoanalysis and individual psychology so that I could learn from listening to my patients. I wanted to find out how they managed to improve their conditions. I began to improvise.

I easily remembered what patients told me, but I often forgot what I told them. So it happened repeatedly that I heard from my patients how they had practiced paradoxical intention. When I asked them how they happened to think of such tricks to fight their neuroses, they were surprised and answered: "Why, it was you who told me." I had forgotten my own invention.

The Years of Medical Apprenticeship

After graduation I first worked under Pötzl in the University Psychiatric Clinic, then for two years with Josef Gerstmann (after whom the "Gerstmann syndrome" or angularis syndrome is named), and in this way I gained experience in neurology. Finally I worked for four years in the mental hospital *Am Steinhof* of which I have spoken. There I was in charge of the "pavilion for suicidal women." At the time I was responsible for no less than 3000 patients each year. This certainly helped to sharpen my diagnostic skills.

While working at Steinhof, I developed my theory of the corrugator phenomenon[35] as a symptom of violent schizophrenic attacks. I recorded my observations in a film that I showed when I gave a short lecture to the Vienna Psychiatric Society on the topic.

My first few days at Steinhof were terrible, and the nights even worse. I was plagued by nightmares associated with dealing with psychotic illnesses. My superior, Leopold Pawlicki,[36] father of the well-known Viennese musician, warned me the first day never to enter the psychotic women's pavilion wearing eyeglasses. I might be hit in the face and splinters of glass could injure my eyes. Such injury, caused by my own carelessness, would not be covered by insurance. I followed this advice and, because I did not see well without my glasses, I was hit in the face the very first day. From then on I wore my glasses and thus could spot any woman who approached, ready to attack me. Thanks to my glasses, I could take to my heels in time.

During my four years at Steinhof I noted in shorthand some amusing sayings of patients. I even toyed with the idea of writing a book with the title, "Fools Tell the Truth." We have a proverb in German that says, "Children and fools tell the truth." I used a few of these stories in my books. For example, an older woman patient was asked this standard question on an IQ test: What is the difference between a child and a dwarf? She answered: "Oh, my. A child is a child, and a dwarf works in a mine." Some of my favorites are answers I received in response to the question, "Are you sexually active now, or have you been in the past?" One patient first said no, but when I asked, "Never?" the response was, "Well yes, as a child." Another woman answered: "You know, doctor, only when I get raped. I don't get around much."

May I mention that the intended book title, "Fools Tell the Truth," also was to point to a theory on which logotherapy—in its original battle against the psychologism of psychotherapy—is based: that what is sick is not necessarily wrong. This theory I have come to call "logotheory." Logotherapy declares war on pathologism. As I have said, two times two make four, even if a paranoid patient says it.

In 1937 I opened my private practice as a specialist in neurology and psychiatry. And this reminds me of an episode. Early in my practice I had a difficult patient. My consulting room was in my parents' home, and they and my siblings were away on vacation. I was alone in the apartment with a big, young, athletic man who was schizophrenic. We lived on the fourth floor, and the windows were open. Suddenly he flew into a rage, swore and cursed at me and threatened to throw me out of the window into the courtyard below. I was not nearly strong enough to resist him. But I didn't beg for my life, or for anything. Rather, I pretended to be deeply offended. "Look here," I said, "that really hurts me to the core. Here I make every effort to help you, and what do I get? You break up our friendship, and I did not expect that from you. It really hurts."

That stopped him, and I was able to persuade him to seek protection from his "enemies" in a clinic. Only there, I told him, and nowhere else would he be safe from them. He then let me take him to a taxi stand. On the way to the stand I convinced him that he should not have to pay money because of the meanness of his enemies. I suggested that he take the taxi, not to the clinic, but directly to the police station. The police would take him to the clinic at the city's expense, where he then would be treated at the expense of the state.

The "Anschluss" of Austria

It was not granted to me to continue my private practice for long. A few months after I had opened it, in March 1938, Hitler's troops marched into Austria. On this politically fateful evening I was lecturing for a colleague for whom I substituted. The title of the lecture was, "Nervousness as a Phenomenon of our Time." Suddenly the door was flung open, and an SA man stood there in Nazi uniform. Could something like that happen under our Chancellor Schuschnigg[37]?, I asked myself. Obviously the SA man intended to disturb the event and force an end to my lecture.

I thought to myself, "I should make the impossible possible, and lecture in such a way that he will forget why he came here. Divert his attention!" So I faced him openly and kept on speaking. He remained at the doorway, not budging from his spot, until I had finished my lecture. This was the act of rhetorical bravery of my life!

I hurried home. The streets were filled with singing, cheering, howling demonstrators. At home I found mother crying; Schuschnigg had just bidden farewell to the Austrian people over the radio, and a sad melody was now being played on the air.

After the entry of Hitler's troops it seemed that everything was jinxed. It was impossible to get a visa for any country. However, when I was offered the chief of neurology position at Rothschild Hospital, I accepted it. The post afforded me and my aging parents a measure of protection from deportation to the concentration camps.

Under the emergency situation of that time, at Rothschild I had the opportunity to make some scientific interventions with dying patients. Up to ten suicide attempts came in every day—so catastrophic was the mood of the

Hitler's triumphant march into Vienna (top) and the mass rally in front of the Chancellor's Office, March 15, 1938 (bottom).

Frankl (center) and his staff of the Rothschild Hospital (1940).

Jewish population in Vienna! To patients who were considered hopeless by the interns, especially by Professor Donath, I gave various stimulants intravenously and, if this did not help, then intracisternally. Even during the war, and with the approval of the consultant for Jewish affairs of the National Socialist medical division, I was able to publish an article about this method in the Swiss journal *Ars Medici.*

At that time I also developed a certain technique of suboccipital brain puncture—a technique that enabled me to eliminate a typical source of danger that I had discovered. As a last resort, when intracisternal injections had no effect, I started to trepan[38] the skull and instill the medication in a side ventricle, while draining the fourth ventricle with a suboccipital puncture. This brought the medication as quickly as possible into the flow direction of the *aqueductus sylvii,* where it could speed up the effect in the vital centers close by. In fact, even patients who had stopped breathing and who had no palpable pulse could be kept alive, and some regained their vital functions to the extent that they began to hyperventilate. Others lived only a day or two longer, but we did what we could.

It should be noted that I could acquire the techniques of brain surgery only from books, mostly from the "Dandy,"[39] a medical text. Professor Reich, the Rothschild Hospital surgeon, refused to perform the operations and Professor Schönbauer—at that time the only expert in brain surgery in Vienna—did not allow me even to watch when he or his staff did brain surgery.

I was so engrossed in brain surgery that I dreamed entire operations. An operating room attendant at Rothschild, who had worked for years with Schönbauer, could not believe it when I told him I had never before worked as a brain surgeon.

My assistant, Dr. Rappaport, protested my efforts to save people who had attempted suicide. Then the day came when she herself received the order for deportation. She attempted suicide, was taken to my department, and I helped to restore her to life. But eventually she was deported.

I do respect the decision of people to end their lives. But I also wish others respect the principle that I have to save lives as long as I am able. I broke this principle only once. An older married couple had attempted double suicide and were brought to Rothschild. The wife had died, and the husband was dying. I was asked whether I should attempt to save him. I did not find it in my heart to do so when I asked myself if I could justify calling the man back to life just so he could attend the funeral of his wife.

There are also people, of course, who know they are incurably ill, that they have not long to live, and that they will only suffer. But even this suffering gives them a chance, an ultimate possibility, to actualize themselves. One can and must show them, with utmost caution, this fundamental possibility. But such heroism for self-actualization may be demanded by one person only—oneself. It is fully as problematic for anyone to insist that *someone else* should have gone to the concentration camp rather than give in to the Nazis. Even if this is so, such a demand can be made only by those who themselves showed such bravery, and not by those who had fled to safety abroad. It is easy to judge people by hindsight.

The perilous medical situation of the Jews under Hitler did have a tragicomical element, as extreme situations often do. Many of the Jewish physicians, including those serving in Vienna's emergency rooms, had been dismissed and deported. They were replaced by young and inexperienced Nazi doctors, which explains the following episode. A patient was taken to Rothschild and pronounced dead by an emergency room physician. She was transferred to the hospital morgue. There she came to life again and went into a fit of madness. She had to be subdued and restrained, and was placed on the internal medicine ward. I suppose this was a rather unusual case in which a patient was transferred from the morgue to internal medicine.

Another sad situation was not without a comical aspect. Thanks to medication, I had helped to free a young epileptic patient from his seizures. In their place, however, he experienced fits of rage. While having such a fit, he stood in the middle of Rotenstern Street, in Vienna's mainly Jewish district, and unleashed a tirade against Hitler in full view of all the people there. I immediately took him off the medication. Soon his seizures erupted again, but he was spared the far more dangerous side effect that had led him to denounce Hitler publicly.

Resisting Euthanasia

Dr. Pötzl, as a party member, wore a swastika on his lapel but he was far from being anti-Semitic. He showed considerable courage and, as much as he could, helped me and my Jewish patients—the only patients I was permitted to treat at the time. Not only did he come to me at the Jewish hospital to order the transfer of brain tumor patients to the surgery unit of the University Clinic, but more than that, he actually helped us sabotage the Nazi orders for euthanasia for the mentally ill.

I had found, at the Jewish home for the aged, a few beds with protective bars and netting that were used in those days. The Gestapo enforced strict compliance with the law that prohibited placing the mentally ill into such homes. I circumvented that law by certifying schizophrenia as aphasia (an organic brain disease) and melancholia as fever delirium (not a psychosis in the strict sense of the word). This protected the administrators of the home, though it put a noose around my own neck. Once the patient was placed inside the protective bars and netting on the bed, schizophrenia could be treated with cardiazol shocks[40] or a phase of melancholia could be overcome without suicide risk.

Pötzl must have gotten wind of it, because thereafter whenever his clinic had a Jewish patient, they phoned the home for the aged: "We have a Jewish patient—will you take him?" Carefully and deliberately they avoided the diagnosis of schizophrenia. They wanted to make use of my diagnostic trickery, and, if someone wanted to sabotage euthanasia, this was a way to do it. The outcome was that members of the National Socialist Party became victims of the euthanasia law while many Jewish patients in the same situation escaped it. Without Pötzl this would have been impossible.

I remember having to pick up a Jewish man and woman who could no longer remain in the private care of a married couple. With me was a social worker from the Jewish Community Center. On the way back two taxis were ahead of us, each transporting a patient. At one point I noticed that one taxi drove on in our direction toward the home, while the other made a left turn.

"How come?" I asked the social worker.

"Oh, yes," she said. "I forgot to tell you. The woman who was taken to the left is no longer Jewish. She converted some time ago, so we are not allowed to accept her at the home for the aged. Unfortunately, she must be taken to the Steinhof mental hospital."

What a crossroad! Straight ahead the safety of the old folks' home, and to the left the road leads via Steinhof to the gas chamber! Who could have foreseen what would result from this woman's decision, for whatever reason, to be converted. A shiver ran down my spine when I realized what circumstances can turn into a death sentence.

The Immigration Visa

I had to wait for years until my quota number came up by which I would be permitted to emigrate to the United States. Finally, shortly before Pearl Harbor, I was asked to come to the American Consulate to pick up my visa. Then I hesitated. Should I leave my parents behind? I knew what their fate would be: deportation to a concentration camp. Should I say goodbye, and leave them to their fate? The visa applied to me alone.

Undecided, I left home, took a walk, and had this thought: "Isn't this the kind of situation that requires some hint from heaven?" When I returned home, my eyes fell on a little piece of marble lying on the table.

"What's this?" I asked my father.

"This? Oh, I picked it out of the rubble of the synagogue they have burned down. It has on it part of the Ten Commandments. I can even tell you from which commandment it comes. There is only one commandment that uses the letter that is chiseled here."

"And that is . . .?" I asked eagerly.

Then father gave me this answer: "Honor thy father and thy mother, that thy days may be long upon the land which the Lord thy God giveth thee."

Thus I stayed "upon the land" with my parents, and let the visa lapse.

It may be that I had made my decision deep within, long before, and that the oracle was in reality only an echo from the voice of my conscience. This is to say, it may have been a kind of projective test. Someone else may have seen in the same piece of marble nothing but $CaCO_3$ (calcium carbonate). But would that not have been his projective test also, perhaps in his case of existential emptiness?

From this I would like to share the story of how I once used a psychotherapeutic technique to postpone the deportation of my parents and myself for perhaps a year. One morning I was awakened by the telephone—the Gestapo. I was to report to their headquarters at a specified time. I asked: "Shall I bring a second set of clothes?"

"Yes," came the answer, and that meant that I would be sent to a concentration camp, that I would never return home. I reported to headquarters and was questioned by an SS man. He wanted to know some details about a man who had fled abroad after committing espionage. I told him that I knew the man by name, but that I had never met him. Then he asked me: "You are a psychiatrist, aren't you? How do you treat agoraphobia? I have a friend who has agoraphobia. What can I tell him?"

I answered: "Tell him, whenever he has an attack of his phobia, he should say to himself: 'I am afraid I could collapse on the street. Fine then, that is exactly what I want. I will collapse and a crowd will gather around me. Worse than that, I will have a heart attack and a stroke to boot, and so on and so forth.'" In short, I instructed him how to use paradoxical intention—for "his friend." Soon I had guessed, of course, that he had been asking for himself.

Be that as it may, this (indirect) logotherapeutic procedure must have worked. Otherwise I cannot explain why my parents and I were spared deportation to the concentration camps for as much as a year.

Tilly

While still in Vienna, it was at the hospital that I met my first wife, Tilly Grosser. She was a station nurse with Professor Donath. I had noticed her because she looked to me like a Spanish dancer. But what really brought us together was her wish to take revenge for her best friend, whom I had dated but then dropped. I had guessed her motive and told her at once. That obviously impressed her.

Beyond that I should say that the decisive part of our mutual relationship was not what one might expect. I did not marry her because she was pretty, nor did she marry

Tilly Frankl.

me because I was "so smart"—and we felt good that these were not our motives.

Of course I was impressed by Tilly's beauty, but her character was the real deciding factor—her natural intuition, her understanding heart. To give one example: Tilly's mother had the benefit of protection from deportation to the camps because Tilly was a station nurse. One day a new regulation came out that canceled this protection for family members. Just before midnight of the day the cancellation took effect, the doorbell rang. Tilly and I were just visiting her mother. But nobody had the courage to answer the door, since we feared it was the pick-up for deportation. Finally, one of us opened, and who stood at the door? A messenger from the Jewish Community Service, asking Tilly's mother to start a new job the next morning—clearing out furniture from the dwellings of just-deported Jews. He also handed her a certificate extending her protection from deportation.

The messenger left, and the three of us sat there looking—no, beaming—at each other. The first to find words was Tilly, and what did she say? "Well, isn't God something!" This was the most beautiful and certainly the shortest *summa theologiae* (to speak with Thomas Aquinas) I had ever heard.

But what finally made me decide to marry Tilly? One day she was preparing the noon meal in my parents' apartment when the phone rang. It was the Rothschild Hospital with an emergency call. A patient had been brought in after a suicide attempt using sleeping pills, and couldn't I try my brain-surgery magic? I didn't even wait to have fresh coffee, but popped a few coffee beans in my mouth to chew while I rushed to the taxi stand, although it was forbidden for Jews to hail taxis.

Two hours later I returned, but the chance for lunch together had passed. I assumed the others had eaten which, in fact, my parents had done. But Tilly had waited, and her first reaction was not, "Finally you're back. I've been holding lunch for you," but rather: "How did it go? How is the patient?" In this moment I decided that I wanted her as my wife. Not because she was this or that. But because she was she.

We were already in the concentration camp when I gave her, for her 23rd birthday I believe, a little trifle that

I had been able to get. I gave it to her with a card on which I had written: "On this your special day, I wish for myself that you be ever true to yourself." A double paradox: for her birthday I wished something for myself, and not for her; and what I wished was that she keep faithful, not to me, but to herself.

When we were married, together with one other couple, we were the last of the Viennese Jews to obtain permission from the National Socialist authorities to wed. After that, the Jewish registrar's office was dissolved. The other couple were my high school history teacher of 20 years earlier, Dr. Edelmann, and his bride.

Not officially, but *de facto*, Jews were forbidden to have children, even couples who were legally married. A decree went around that from now on pregnant Jewish women would be deported immediately to a concentration camp. The Medical Society was instructed not to interfere with abortions on Jewish women. Tilly had to sacrifice the fetus she was carrying. My book, *The Unheard Cry for Meaning*, is dedicated to this, our unborn child.

After our wedding ceremony at the Jewish Community Center under a *chuppe*, the traditional Jewish canopy, we could not take a taxi since it was forbidden to Jews, but had to walk through the streets of Vienna for the usual photographs: Tilly in her white bridal veil. Then we walked home and past a bookstore that showed in its window a book with the title, *We Want to Get Married*. After a long hesitation we dared to enter, Tilly still in her veil, and both of us wearing the yellow Jewish stars. I got a kick out of making her ask for the book. I wanted to encourage her self-assertion. And so there she stood: white veil, yellow star on her dress, and in response to the sales clerk's question about what she would like, she said with a blush: "We Want to Get Married."

Wedding photo of Frankl with his first wife, Tilly (1941).

Our wedding photo came to my aid unexpectedly after the war. I was the first Austrian permitted by occupying forces to travel abroad, to give a lecture at a conference in Switzerland. From Innsbruck I telegraphed my hosts in Zurich—friends of Tilly's family whom I had never met—to meet me at the train station. So that they could recognize me, I told them I would be wearing on my coat a red triangle standing on its point. This was the emblem that we Jews had been required to wear in the concentration camps.

At Zurich I waited for someone to meet me. Finally, a female figure appeared from the mist, approached me slowly and haltingly, holding a photo in her hand that she kept comparing with me.

"Are you Dr. Frankl?" she asked me. Then I saw that she held a copy of our wedding photo, which showed me with Tilly in her bridal veil. Fortunately my host had brought the photo along, or she never would have found me. There were hordes of people at the station with red triangles in their buttonholes. As it happened, on the same evening, volunteers had been collecting money for the "winter assistance" program, which supplied basic food and coal for heat to the most needy citizens. Everyone who dropped a coin in the collection box received, as a sign of payment, a red triangle standing on its point. And *these* red triangles were larger and even more conspicuous than mine.

The Concentration Camps

Nine months after our wedding we were at Theresienstadt, a concentration camp less reprehensible than most. There Tilly was granted a two-year exemption from transfer to Auschwitz because she was working in a munitions factory, which was important to the war effort. I, however, was called up for "Transport East" and we assumed that this meant Auschwitz. I knew Tilly well, and I was sure that she would do her utmost to go with me. So I enjoined her ardently that she should *not* volunteer to join my transport. To do so would be dangerous for more than one reason; it could also be interpreted as her way of undermining war production. Despite all of this and without my knowledge, Tilly did volunteer and, for whatever reasons, was approved for transport.

During the transport she was true to herself. After a brief spell of panic, when she cried, "You'll see. We are heading for Auschwitz," she suddenly became quite calm again. In the crowded freight car she began to sort out the jumbled luggage and engaged others to help her.

In the last minutes we were together at Auschwitz she was outwardly serene. Just before we parted, she whispered to me that she had smashed a clock (an alarm clock, as I remember it) so that the SS wouldn't get it. And she obviously relished this tiny triumph. As the men and women were being separated I told her, in the firmest tone possible so that she could not miss what I was saying, "Tilly, stay alive at any price. Do you hear? At any price!"

I was trying to tell her that, if she found herself in a situation where she could save her life only at the price of yielding sexually, she should not feel inhibited out of any consideration for me. By giving her, so to speak, an absolution in advance, I was hoping to spare myself the guilt if such an inhibition might lead to her death.

Shortly after my liberation from Türkheim near Munich, I was walking across a field when I met a Dutch laborer. Now, after his own liberation, he was a displaced person. As he and I were talking, he kept playing with a small object in his hands.

"What do you have there?" I asked him.

He opened his palm, and there I saw a tiny golden globe, the oceans painted in blue enamel, with a gold band for the equator. On it this inscription: "The whole world turns on love." It was a pendant—*a pendant*? It was just like the one I had given to Tilly on her first birthday that we celebrated together. Just like it? It could have been the very pendant, for when I bought it I was told that there existed only two of its kind in Vienna. And in Bad Wörishofen, near Türkheim, a storehouse was discovered where the SS had stored an enormous collection of jewelry that came from the extermination camps, which means that Auschwitz was the primary source. I bought the pendant from the man. It was dented slightly, but the whole world still turned on love.

One more recollection related to this. It was on the very first morning of my return to Vienna, in August 1945, that I learned that Tilly had died with many others after the liberation of Bergen–Belsen by English soldiers. They had discovered 17,000 corpses and, during the following six weeks, another 17,000 prisoners died from sickness, starvation, and exhaustion. Tilly must have been among them.

Deportation

Permit me to circle back to the time of my deportation. As the situation in Vienna grew more ominous, and I was expecting to be deported with my parents, I sat down and wrote a first draft of *Ärztliche Seelsorge* [*The Doctor and the Soul*]. I thought that at least the essentials of logotherapy should survive me.

Later, upon my arrival at Auschwitz, the manuscript was sewn into the lining of my overcoat, hidden there. Of course it was lost when I had to throw everything on the ground: my clothing, my last few belongings, and my pride and joy, the badge of the Donauland Alpine Club, which certified me as a climbing guide.

At Theresienstadt, Hitler's "model ghetto," I had been placed for a time in the so-called "Little Fortress" on

Frankl (far left) with his rock-climbing companions from the Donauland Alpine Club.

the periphery of the camp. Here, even before Auschwitz, I got a bitter taste of "a real concentration camp." After a few hours of labor, I was dragged back to my barracks with 31 wounds of varying severity, dragged by a Viennese rascal—a petty criminal (of whom I shall say more in another episode I shall describe later). On the way back, Tilly saw me and rushed to my side.

"For heavens sake, what have they done to you?" In the barrack she, the trained nurse, bandaged me and took care of me. That evening, when I had recovered somewhat, she wanted to divert my attention from my misery. So she took me to another barrack where a jazz band, known in Prague, was playing—without official permission. They played a tune that was the unofficial "national anthem" of the Jews in Theresienstadt: *"Bei mir bist du schön"* ["To me, you are beautiful"].

The contrast between the indescribable tortures of the morning and the jazz in the evening was typical of our existence—with all its contradictions of beauty and hideousness, humanity and inhumanity.

Auschwitz

Until now, I have never published the story of what happened at the "first selection" at the Auschwitz railroad station. This is partly because I sometimes wonder if I must have imagined it. This was the situation.

Dr. Joseph Mengele, one of the Holocaust's most notorious mass murderers, was selecting prisoners: to the right for labor in the camps, and to the left for the gas chambers. In my case, Mengele pointed my shoulder toward the left. Since I recognized no one in the left line, behind Mengele's back I switched over to the right line where I saw a few of my young colleagues. Only God knows where I got that idea or found the courage.

Entering Auschwitz, when I was required to discard my own, perfectly good coat, I took an old, torn one. It had apparently belonged to a person who had been gassed. In a pocket I found a leaf, torn from a prayer

The infamous Doctor Mengele at the station of Auschwitz during the "selection."

book. On this scrap of paper was the principal prayer of Judaism, the *Shema Israel* ("Hear, oh Israel, the Lord our God is One"). How else could I interpret this "coincidence" than as a challenge to me *to live* what I had written, to practice what I had preached? From that point on, that prayer book page stayed with me, hidden in the lining of my coat (as my lost manuscript had been). I get an uncanny sense when I think how I was able to save— back into freedom—the bits of paper on which I had reconstructed my book manuscript; yet the scrap from the prayer book inexplicably vanished at the time of my liberation.

Earlier I mentioned a Viennese rascal. Along with other rowdies and criminals he had become a Capo, an inmate chosen by the camp administration to help keep order among the prisoners. One day the following episode took place.

I was the last one to be put into a group of 100 earmarked for transport. Just as our group was about to be moved forward, this rascal pounced on another inmate who was standing nearby and began to beat him with a barrage of body blows. Then he literally kicked the inmate into our group, at the same time grabbing me and pulling me out. He cursed the beaten prisoner with a flood of filthy profanities, and made it appear that he had tried to slip out of the group. By the time I realized what was happening, the 100 men were already being marched off without me. The rascal—my protector, in this case—must have known that the group was ill-fated, perhaps destined for the gas chambers. (Now I am convinced that this scalawag saved my life).

Later, in the camp Kaufering III, Benscher, the Munich television actor-to-be, also saved my life. I swapped a cigarette for a cup of watery soup that at least had the odor of smoked meat. While I was sipping the soup, he talked to me with great urgency, imploring me to get over my pessimism. The mood that had overcome me was the mood I had observed in other inmates, which almost inevitably led to giving up and, sooner or later, to death.

When I came down with typhus in the Türkheim camp, I was near death. I kept thinking that my book would never be published. But I brought myself to face up to this question: "What kind of life would it be, whose meaning depends entirely on whether a book gets published?" In the Hebrew Bible, after Abraham was prepared to sacrifice his only son, a ram was caught in the underbrush. It seemed to me, in my situation, that I had to bring myself to be ready to sacrifice my book, a kind of

*(Top) Charred corpses of inmates of the concentration camp
Kaufering III after the camp was set on fire by the fleeing SS men at
the end of the war. (The photo was taken by an officer of the U.S. army
whose troops had liberated the camp.) (bottom) The half-subterranean
barracks of camp Kaufering III.*

spiritual child for me, in order to be judged worthy of its eventual publication—*The Doctor and the Soul.*

After surviving the typhus attack, it was especially at night that I experienced strange breathing difficulties, including painful respiration. I was desperate and decided, in the middle of the night, to go to the barrack of the head physician of the camp, my Hungarian colleague Dr. Racz, himself an inmate. I will never forget how I had to crawl in total darkness across the 100 yards between my barrack and his. This was strictly forbidden at night, and I was aware that the guard in the watchtower might spot and shoot me with his machine gun. I had a choice in the risk of death: to choke or to be shot.

I never had nightmares about those rigorous final exams in high school, as many Austrian students did. These finals are called the *Matura* in Vienna—a test of maturation. But I still have nightmares about life in the concentration camps; this was the true test of my maturation. Actually, I could have escaped these *Matura* exams if I had emigrated to America. There I could have developed logotherapy; there I could have finished my life's work, fulfilled my task. But I did not emigrate, and so I ended up at Auschwitz. It was the *experimentum crucis.* The two basic human capacities, self-transcendence and self-distancing, were verified and validated in the concentration camps.

This experiential evidence confirms the survival value of "the will to meaning" and of self-transcendence—the reaching out beyond ourselves for something other than ourselves. Under the same conditions, those who were oriented toward the future, toward a meaning that waited to be fulfilled—these persons were more likely to survive. Nardini and Lifton, two American military psychiatrists, found the same to be the case in the prisoner-of-war camps in Japan and Korea.

I am convinced that I owe my survival, among other things, to my resolve to reconstruct that lost manuscript. I started to work on it when I was sick with typhus and tried to keep awake, even in the night, to prevent a vascular collapse. For my 40th birthday an inmate had given me a pencil stub, and almost miraculously he had pilfered a few small SS forms. On the backs of these forms I scribbled notes that might help me reconstruct *The Doctor and the Soul*.

The notes actually served me well when I later started to fulfill my hopes by committing to paper the second draft of that first book, now enriched by the confirmation of my theory in the concentration camps. There, in the camp, I had already drafted an additional chapter on the psychology of the camps.

At the First International Congress for Psychotherapy in Leiden, Holland, I disclosed to the audience how I had used self-distancing:

> I repeatedly tried to distance myself from the misery that surrounded me by externalizing it. I remember marching one morning from the camp to the work site, hardly able to bear the hunger, the cold, and the pain of my frozen and festering feet, so swollen from hunger edema and squeezed into my shoes. My situation seemed bleak, even hopeless. Then I imagined that I stood at the lectern in a large, beautiful, warm and bright hall. I was about to give a lecture to an interested audience on, "Psychotherapeutic Experiences in a Concentration Camp" (the actual title I later used at that congress[41]). In the imaginary lecture I reported the things that I am now living through. Believe me, ladies and gentlemen, at that moment I could not dare to hope that some day it would be my good fortune to actually give such a lecture.

I spent a total of three years in four camps: Theresienstadt, Auschwitz, Kaufering III, and Türkheim. I survived.

SS forms on whose backs Frankl scribbled shorthand notes to reconstruct the manuscript of Ärztliche Seelsorge, which had been destroyed in Auschwitz.

But as for my family, except for my sister who had gone to Australia, one might say as did Rilke: "The Lord gave everyone his own death." My father died in Theresienstadt practically in my arms. My mother died in the gas chambers of Auschwitz. My brother, so I was told, perished in a mine of one of the branch camps of Auschwitz.

The gravestone in memory of members of the Frankl family who perished in various concentration camps.

My old friend Erna Felmayer some time ago sent me a poem I had written on the back of a prescription in 1946, which shows my mood at the time:

> You weigh on me, you whom I lost in death.
> You've given me the silent charge to live for you;
> So it is for me now to erase the debt of your extermination.
> Until I know that with each ray of sun
> You wish to warm me and to meet me;
> Until I see that in each blossoming tree
> There's someone dead who wants to greet me;
> Until I hear that every bird's song is your voice
> Sounding out to bless me and perhaps to say
> That you forgive me that I live.

When the mayor of Austin, Texas, made me an honorary citizen of that city, I replied:

> It really is not appropriate that you make me an honorary citizen. It would be more fitting if I make you an honorary logotherapist. Had not so many young soldiers from Texas, among them several from your city, risked and even sacrificed their lives, there would be no Frankl and no logotherapy today. You see, it was your Texas soldiers who liberated me and many others from the camp at Türkheim.[42]

The mayor's eyes were filled with tears.

When I had returned to Vienna after my liberation, again and again I had to listen to the question, "Didn't they do enough to you in this city, to you and to your family?" I answered with a counter-question: "Who did what to me?" There had been a Catholic baroness who risked her life by hiding my cousin for years in her apartment. There had been a Socialist attorney (Bruno Pitterman, later vice chancellor of Austria), who knew me only

Frankl, with his wife Elly and the mayor of Austin, after being named honorary citizen of the capital of Texas.

casually and for whom I had never done anything; and it was he who smuggled some food to me whenever he could. For what reason, then, should I turn my back on Vienna?

Collective Guilt

Those who propound the concept of collective guilt are mistaken. Whenever possible I have fought this idea, and in *Man's Search for Meaning,* my book about the concentration camps, I tell the following story:

The head of the camp from which I was liberated was an SS man. After liberation we heard what, up to then, only the camp physician (himself an inmate) knew. This SS man had secretly spent considerable sums of his own money at the drug store in the nearby village, purchasing medications for the camp inmates.

The story has a sequel. Jewish prisoners, after their liberation, hid this SS man from the American troops and told the commanding officer that they would deliver him only on condition that no harm would come to him. The American commander gave his word of honor, and the former inmates turned in the SS man. The commander reappointed him, as it were, this time to organize the collection of food and clothing for us in the surrounding villages.

In 1946 it was intensely unpopular to take a stand against collective guilt, or to defend some National Socialists, as I have done. In doing so I drew reprimands from various organizations. I hid a medical colleague in my apartment, thus protecting him from prosecution by the authorities simply for having received a badge of honor from the Hitler Youth organization. He would have faced a trial at a special court for Nazi crimes, with sentences restricted to two: acquittal or capital punishment.

In 1946, I lectured in the French occupation zone of Austria. I spoke against collective guilt in the presence of the commanding general of the French forces. The next day a university professor came to me, himself a former SS officer, with tears in his eyes. He asked how I could find the courage to take an open stand against collective guilt. "*You* can't do it," I told him. "You would be speaking out of self-interest. But *I* am the former inmate number 119104, and I *can* do it. Therefore I *must*. People will listen to me, and so it is my obligation to speak against it."

Vienna: My Return and My Writing

While I was still in the camp, I promised myself that I would look for Professor Pötzl if I ever should make it back to Vienna. And so the first thing I did on my arrival there was to find him. Just before I visited him I learned that my first wife, Tilly, had lost her life. Pötzl, my old teacher, was the first one on whose shoulder I could weep out my grief. But there was no way that I could be of help to *him*. As a former member of the Nazi party, he had been fired from his post that same day, and without recourse. But, as my other friends, he feared for my life—worried that I might commit suicide.

It was Bruno Pittermann who compelled me to sign a blank form which he later used as the application for a vacant position at the Vienna Policlinic Hospital. (For the next 25 years I was head of its neurology department.)

On one of those first days back in Vienna, I looked up my friend Paul Polak and told him about the deaths of my parents, my brother, and Tilly. I remember that I burst into tears and said: "Paul, I must tell you, that when all this happens to someone, to be tested in such a way, that it must have some meaning. I have a feeling—and I don't know how else to say it—that something waits for me. That something is expected of me, that I am destined for something." After this I felt relieved, and no one could have understood me better than my dear old friend, Paul Polak.

Otto Kauders, Pötzl's successor as chief of psychiatry at the University Clinic, urged me to write the third and last draft of *The Doctor and the Soul*, and to use it to fulfill one of the requirements for becoming a university lecturer. This was the only thing that seemed worthwhile to me, and I buried myself in work.

I dictated and dictated. Three stenographer-typists worked in shifts to capture it all, so much poured out of my heart every day. This was in unheated, sparsely furnished rooms, where the broken windows were covered with cardboard. Words gushed from my lips as I paced about the room. Now and then—I see it still—I collapsed into a chair, weeping. So moved was I by thoughts that of-

Frankl, 1946.

ten overwhelmed me with painful vividness. The flood-gates had opened.

That same year I dictated *Man's Search for Meaning* in nine days. As I dictated, I decided that this book about the concentration camps should be published anonymously, so that I could express myself freely. The cover of the first edition does not identify an author. The manuscript was at the printers when friends persuaded me to avow the contents with my name. I could not resist their appeal for courage or their argument that I should accept my responsibility.

Is it not strange that, among all my books, this is the one I wrote believing that it should be published anonymously and that it should never bring me personal recognition? This is the book that has now been translated into

The Policlinic Hospital in Vienna's ninth district.

Frankl in the lecture hall of the Policlinic in 1948, making a lumbar puncture on a patient.

24 languages. It has been chosen five times by American colleges as "the book of the year."

At Baker University, in Kansas, the entire curriculum for three years was given the theme and the title of the book. I know of a Trappist monastery where, for a time, passages from this little book were read in the refec-

Cover of the first edition of Ein Psycholog erlebt das KZ, *later retitled*...trotzdem Ja zum Leben sagen *[Say Yes to Life in Spite of Everything],* English version Man's Search for Meaning. *The sketch of the cover was suggested by Frankl, based on a personal experience.*

tory at the noon meal. At a Catholic church the same was done during Mass, and in another place nuns printed quotations on bookmarks for their students. A university professor gave his philosophy students an assignment with this title: "What would Socrates and Frankl have discussed if they had shared the same prison cell?"

It is touching to see how receptive America's young people are to this book, though I cannot explain their response to it. On the instigation of Gordon Allport, who wrote the preface, I added a second more theoretical part,

"Logotherapy in a Nutshell." This is a distillation of logo-therapy, while the first part is the autobiographical account of my experience in the camps. Each part strengthens and complements the other.

It is perhaps a good sign that, even in this day of advertising and marketing pressures, a book can make its way. The publisher of the English edition would never have printed the book at all, had it not been for the effort of Gordon Allport. Even with that, the paperback rights were peddled from one publisher to another and finally sold for $200—and the buyer, unexpectedly, made a huge profit.

Ärztliche Seelsorge was discovered by an American commission combing through Europe after the war to find books worth translating. It was the only one by an Austrian author that was chosen, and that is how *The Doctor and the Soul* made it into English.

Sometimes comical situations develop in the making of books. A Portuguese publisher wrote to me that he wanted to take on *Man's Search for Meaning* in his language. I reminded him that he had already published it years earlier. The publicity he had provided for my book apparently never even reached his editors. Another publisher, in Norway, informed me regretfully that he was declining a certain book of mine—not realizing that he had already published it.

In 1945, when I wrote these first two books, I never dreamed that they would find such a reception abroad. And writing many other books since has become part of this personally satisfying endeavor. Yet as I look back, the most rewarding hour for me was delivering the final version of *Ärztliche Seelsorge* to my very first publisher, Franz Deuticke in Vienna. He was Freud's first publisher as well.

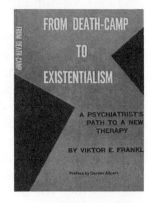

Some of Frankl's books.

The Frankls on the Rax Mountain.

Speaking and talking come easy to me, but not writing. To do it has required many sacrifices, always shared by my wife. I have stayed at home, at my desk, through many a radiant, sunny Sunday, refining my manuscripts when I would have loved to go climbing in the mountains.

The sacrifices of Elly may be even greater than my own. So that I might complete my life's work, she has denied herself much. She is the counterpart to me, both quantitatively and qualitatively. What I accomplish with my brain she fulfills with her heart. Jacob Needleman once said, referring to the way in which Elly has been my companion on our lecture tours: "She is the warmth that accompanies the light."

One of my books contains a page that I dictated ten times over, and a sentence that took me three hours to get into final form. During dictation I become so absorbed in my subject that I ignore nearly everything around me. I lose track of time. It happened, for example, that I was lying in bed, completely preoccupied, with dictating machine beside me and microphone in hand. Elly was keenly aware that we had to meet a train in half an hour, so she tiptoed over to me to remind me. My response was: "Elly, comma, please get my bath ready, exclamation point!" Even before she burst out laughing, I realized what I had done.

I have already confessed my perfectionism. But it is the kind of perfectionism Saint-Exupéry referred to when he said: "Perfection does not mean that there is nothing more to add, but that there is nothing more to leave out."

Among the responses to my writings, the most pleasant are often letters from American readers. Hardly a week passes without a letter saying, "Dr. Frankl, your book has changed my life."

One day, shortly after the war, we had a visitor. Elly announced that an Ingenieur Kausel was here and added, "But surely this cannot be the famous Kausel who has just been released from prison." I asked Elly to show him in.

"My name is Kausel. I don't know if you have seen the stories about me in the papers."

Indeed, we had seen them. Everyone had been convinced that he had murdered a woman, and all the evidence seemed against him. By a pure coincidence, the actual murderer had been apprehended.

"What can I do for you, *Herr Ingenieur*?" I asked him.

"Nothing. I just came to thank you. In prison I was in despair—no one would believe in my innocence. But somebody gave me your book, in my cell. It was the only thing that lifted my spirit."

"Really? What do you mean?" I inquired.

He explained that he had seen the challenge to make good his "attitudinal values"—that he could, even in such circumstances, still choose what attitude he would take toward his inescapable predicament. He was quite specific, and by this I could see that he had understood how logotherapy applied to his concrete situation, and that it had helped him.

In Asia there is a dictatorship whose ruler canceled an announced election and threw his opponent into prison. In an interview reported in *Newsweek,* this man explained how he was able to cope with those years in prison: "My mother brought me a book by a Viennese psychologist by the name of Viktor Frankl, and that book keeps me going."

Encounters with Philosophers

Among my most cherished experiences are my discussions with Martin Heidegger[43] when he visited us in Vienna. He wrote in my guest book: "To remember a visit on a beautiful and informative morning." On a photo taken at a typical Viennese wine garden, he wrote a sentence that was meant to point out the kinship between our philosophies: *"Das Vergangene geht, das Gewesene kommt"* [What has passed is gone, what is past will come].

Here, as in many other cases, my experience with great personalities whom I esteemed was that they were gracious toward me. They overlooked the inadequacies of my efforts, always seeing something positive in them—even though they had every right to be critical. This I experienced not only with Heidegger, but also with Ludwig Binswanger,[44] Karl Jaspers,[45] and Gabriel Mar-

Frankl visiting Martin Heidegger.

cel.[46] Marcel, incidentally, wrote the preface to the French edition of *Man's Search for Meaning*.

Karl Jaspers told me, on my visit to Basel: *"Herr Frankl,* I know all of your books, but the one about the concentration camp (pointing to it in his bookcase) belongs among the great books of humankind."

Lectures around the World

In addition to my writing, there are my lectures across the years. I enjoy giving lectures, but the preparation is not easy. When I was planning for my festival address at the 600th anniversary of the University of Vienna, I scribbled

Frankl visiting Karl Jaspers.

Frankl visiting Ludwig Binswanger.

nearly 150 pages of notes. This was no manuscript, and I never use one when speaking—only notes.

It took a while before I dared to speak freely in English, which is not to say that my English is correct even now.

Elly and I typically assume that people in America will not understand my German. But sometimes they do, unexpectedly. In Montreal a customer sat down next to us in a cafeteria and started wiping the table over and over. Then he went to work on the silverware, shining it repeatedly. I said to Elly in German: "Typical obsessive–compulsive behavior, perhaps a severe case of bacteriophobia ...," and who knows what else I said? As we were leaving, I could not find my overcoat right away, and this man addressed us in faultless German: "Are you folks looking for something. Can I be of any help?" It was clear that he had understood every word of my whole psychiatric diagnosis.

These incidents occur often as we travel in other countries. In the 1960s, a boy in California asked me where I was from. "From Vienna," I told him, "do you know where that is?" He said no. I wanted to help him without pointing out his ignorance. "But surely you have heard of the Viennese waltz?"

"Oh, yes, but I haven't learned to dance."

I was not about to give up, so I asked him: "But you do know what a Viennese schnitzel is?"

"I've heard of it," he said, "but I've never danced to it."

As a guest lecturer I have been at more than 200 universities outside of Europe—in the Americas, Australia, Asia, Africa. To the United States alone I have made 92 lecture trips. On four tours Elly and I have gone around the world, one of them in a period of two weeks. Because

Visiting the Eisenhower home upon the invitation of the President's widow Mamie.

we flew east across the international date line, and gained time, I was able to give 15 daily lectures in 14 days. One evening I spoke in Tokyo and the next day in Honolulu, but the date was the same.

It was through my books that Mamie Eisenhower, widow of the American president, knew of me. She sent the family physician and his wife to Vienna to invite us to their estate near Washington.

I learned that Mrs. Eisenhower had asked her staff in Gettysburg how she might prepare for the Frankl visit, but she was assured that no preparations would be necessary. Nevertheless, she asked to see a film of an earlier visit to Vienna. At least she wanted to have some key words and places in mind, such as Belvedere Palace, the giant Ferris wheel, St. Stephen's Cathedral, etc. But she managed without them.

As soon as we met, she asked us to call her "Mamie." She showed us gifts they had received from various heads of state, and especially the gifts that her husband had given her when he was a cadet and during their engagement. They had started out with only a few dollars, and these gifts had become the most precious to her. I have never met, nor can I imagine, a person less self-impressed, or more natural, or more kind to talk with than this First Lady.

In Rome, the Young Presidents Organization rented the Hilton Hotel for their seminars. The three speakers they invited were astronaut Wally Schirra; Otto von Hapsburg, son of the last Austrian emperor; and neurologist Viktor Frankl.

In the United States a lecturer is often judged by the honorarium paid, and this can run to $10,000 or more for a single speech. I mention this to illustrate my attitude toward money. In itself, money matters little to me. One must have some, but the true meaning of money lies in one's ability to spend it without having to worry about it.

In my childhood I was different. As soon as my sister Stella had been given a 10-heller piece by Uncle Erwin, I convinced her that she had swollen tonsils and that I had to operate to remove them. I hid a small red marble in one hand and with the other put some scissors into her mouth. After making some suitable noise, I presented her with the marble as her tonsil. The charge for the surgery was 10-heller. In this way I "earned" money.

Some say time is money. For me, time means much more than money. When the president of Cornell Univer-

The Frankls at the "American Ball" in Vienna's Imperial Castle Schönbrunn. (In the background, far right, Dr. Otto von Hapsburg, the son of Austria's last emperor.)

sity offered me $9,000 for a brief stay on his campus and I declined, he asked: "Is it too little?" "No," I answered, "but if you asked me what I would buy with $9,000, I would say time—time for my work. Since I do not have enough time now for my work, I wouldn't want to sell it to anyone."

When I am convinced that a lecture may be of real importance to an audience, I sometimes offer it without honorarium. I am ready also to forego an agreed-upon fee, as I did in the case of a scheduled lecture to a student body in Ottawa. They failed to collect the funds needed and almost canceled the lecture because of this. Instead, I insisted on giving it without pay.

The outreach of my lectures is difficult to assess, but there are some experiences I remember well. Once I gave a free, "folksy" talk at the University of Vienna. When I arrived at the designated room, people came running out because the talk had to be moved to a larger space. I followed them, but again the room was too small. We ended up in the university festival hall, which accommodated everyone. As early as 1947, I had to repeat a lecture twice at the Vienna Concert Hall because of attendance.

But there are limits on popularity. The Austrian Chancellor's office called to tell me that one of the best known American photographers, Irving Penn, was coming to Vienna to shoot for an American magazine. It was to be a feature on Vienna, and the conductor Karajan, the sculptor Wotruba, and the psychotherapist Frankl would be photographed to go with the story. Presumably, these three Viennese men were of interest to Americans.

The photographer flew in, showed up at our apartment and shot over 400 photographs. He left happily. During the next few months I was in the States several times and checked the latest issues of that magazine. No story about Vienna. Then, finally, it appeared: giant photo fold-outs of the famous Vienna Lippizaner stallions and of whipped-cream tortes, but no photos of Karajan, Wotruba, and Frankl. Apparently we were no competition for horses and pastry.

Frankl, lecturing.

The natural enthusiasm of Latin Americans is difficult for Europeans to grasp. When my wife and I landed in San Juan, capital of Puerto Rico, we were halfway down the gangway when we were stopped. Police barrier. We waited a long time. What was happening? A television crew was looking for two passengers by the name of Frankl, in order to film their arrival reception. Elly and I had already passed through. I suppose we hadn't looked prominent enough.

In another Latin American country, the First Lady there attended all three lectures I gave in one day, each

Portrait taken (in Vienna's Prater Park) by the legendary American photographer Alfred Eisenstaedt.

lasting two hours. Her husband, the president, invited me for breakfast to discuss the cultural situation of his country. Both had read my books. Back home in Europe I dare not tell stories like this one. No one would believe them. So all the more I enjoy writing about these incidents now.

On Aging

I don't mind getting old. As I say, aging doesn't bother me as long as I have reason to believe that I am also ma-

Frankl, at 70, climbing the Lutterwall.

turing. Perhaps this is still going on, since now I see the flaws in a manuscript I finished two weeks ago. Perchance compensation processes are also in play.

I am reminded of what happened when I was climbing the Preiner Cliff on the Rax Mountain. My guide was Naz Gruber, who had once led a Himalayan expedition.

He was sitting there on a rocky overhang, securing me with the rope as I climbed after him. Suddenly he said, "Y'know, professor, when I watch you there climbing—don't be mad, but you don't have a penny's worth of strength left. But you make up for it by your clever climbing technique. I must say, a guy could learn about climbing from you." Well, this from a Himalayan conqueror—how grand I felt when I heard it!

In the last analysis, getting old is an aspect of the transitoriness of human existence. But this transitoriness can be a strong motivation for our responsibleness—our recognition of responsibility as basic to human existence. It may be proper to repeat the logotherapeutic maxim as I formulated it in a dream. I jotted it down when I woke up, and used it in *The Doctor and the Soul*: "Live as if you were already living for the second time, and as if you had made the mistakes you are about to make now." And indeed, one's sense of responsibility can be heightened by such a fictive autobiographical view of one's own life.

Audience with the Pope

I do not deserve to be congratulated for whatever success logotherapy has enjoyed. In a private audience granted to us by Pope Paul VI, I told him: "While others may look at what I may have accomplished, or rather at what turned out well by good fortune, I realize at such moments how much more I should have done, but failed to do. In other words, how much do I owe to God's grace, granted to me for all these years beyond the time I was forced to walk through the gates of Auschwitz."

Private audience with Pope Paul VI.

My wife Elly was with me for the audience with the Pope, and we were both deeply impressed. Pope Paul VI greeted us in German and continued in Italian, with a priest as interpreter. He acknowledged the significance of logotherapy for the Catholic Church and for all of humankind. He also commended my conduct in the concentration camps, but it was unclear to us what he had in mind.

As he signaled the end of the audience, and as we were moving toward the door, he suddenly began to speak in German once again, calling after us—to me, the Jewish neurologist from Vienna—in exactly these words: "Please pray for me!"

It was deeply stirring. We could see in the face of this man the nightly tortures of his struggle with his conscience, as he wrestled with those critical decisions that made him, and the Catholic Church, unpopular. His face was carved with the strain of those restless nights.

I am fully aware of the inadequacies of my efforts, and I have said this before. And also of the bias inherent in logotherapy. Bias is unavoidable, and it was Kierkegaard who once said that anyone who offers a corrective had to be biased, "thoroughly biased." To be self-consciously one-sided in righting a wrong is no vice. Or as I formulated it in my concluding speech at the Fifth International Congress for Psychotherapy in 1961: "As long as we do not have access to absolute truth, we must be contented that our relative truths correct one another, and that we find the courage to be biased. In the many-voiced orchestra of psychotherapy we not only have the right, but the duty to be biased as long as we are conscious of it."

My own bias, about which I am both aware and outspoken, attacks the cynicism for which nihilism is to blame, and the nihilism for which cynicism is responsible. This is a vicious cycle of nihilistic indoctrination and cynical motivation. What is needed to break this cycle is for us to *unmask the unmaskers*—those advocates and practitioners of a thoroughly biased "depth psychology," which prides itself on its powers "to unmask" the dark, unconscious mysteries in persons. Freud has taught us how important the unmasking is. But the unmasking has to stop somewhere, and the place to stop is where the "unmasking psychologist" is confronted with something that *cannot be unmasked for the simple reason that it is genuine*. Those psychologists, however, who do not stop their unmasking even there only disclose their own tendency—be it conscious or unconscious— to devaluate what is genuine, what is truly human, in human beings.

Suffering and Meaning

I have gone through the school of psychologism and the hell of nihilism. It may be that each person who develops his own system of psychotherapy writes, in the final analysis, his own case history. But we must ask ourselves if this therapy also applies to the collective neuroses of our time. This would justify the bearing of our suffering for the sake of others. In a sense, our illness could then help to immunize others.

All this is true not only for the collective neuroses, but for neuroses in general. It is true for all suffering humanity.

The president of the Alfred Adler Institute in Tel Aviv mentioned in a lecture the case of a young Israeli soldier who had lost both legs in the Yom Kippur War. It was not possible to get him over his depression, and he even contemplated suicide. Then, one day she found him completely changed, serene. "What happened to you?" she asked in surprise. He handed her the Hebrew translation of *Man's Search for Meaning* and said: "This book is what happened to me." There may be such a thing as autobibliotherapy—healing through reading—and apparently logotherapy is particularly well suited to it.

Once in a while people write me letters about similar experiences. One of these was a letter that included a large page from a newspaper, complete with photographs. It came from Jerry Long, the clipping from the *Texarkana Gazette* of April 6, 1980. Jerry was 17 when he became the victim of a paralyzing diving accident. He was left a quadriplegic, having lost the use of both arms and legs. He can type only by using a pencil-size rod that he holds in his mouth. With his left shoulder he can operate a conveyance that enables him to participate in a university seminar, part of his studies to become a psychologist. His reason? "I like people and want to help them," he wrote to me. He explained his spontaneous decision to write to me in these words: "I have read with much interest *Man's Search for Meaning*, though my difficulties seem to be far less than those suffered by you and your comrades. Reading your book nevertheless showed me innumerable similarities between them. Even after four readings, new insight and substance are gained each time. Only the man on the inside knows. What a far greater impact your book has because you lived it... I have suffered, but I know that without the suffering, the growth I have achieved would have been impossible." Later, when we met face to face, he told me: "The accident broke my back, but it did not break me."

This elucidates the catalytic effect, not only of "book as therapy" but also of psychotherapy in general. When I speak in lectures and books about techniques versus a human approach, often I have told of a phone call I received around three o'clock in the morning. This woman had decided to end her life, and she was curious about what I had to say. I offered all the arguments against such a step and we discussed the pros and cons. We finally reached the point where she promised to postpone her plans and to come to see me at nine that same morning.

She appeared on time and began: "You would be mistaken, doctor, if you thought that any of your arguments last night had the least impact on me. If anything helped me, it was this. Here I disturb a man's sleep in the middle of the night, and instead of getting angry, he listens patiently to me for half an hour and encourages me.

I thought to myself: If this can happen, then it may be worthwhile to give my life another chance." In this case it was more the human response that helped, not any technique as such.

On another occasion I arrived at the clinic in the morning and was greeted by a small group of American professors, psychiatrists, and students who had come to Vienna to do research. I had just responded to *Who's Who in America* by returning the questionnaire they had sent. It had asked that I express, in one sentence, the meaning of my life. So I asked the group to guess what response I had made. Some quiet reflection. Then a student from Berkeley said, and his answer jolted me: "The meaning of your life is to help others find the meaning of theirs."

That was it, exactly. Those are the very words I had written.

Last, but Far from Least

1946. Surrounded by my medical staff, I made rounds in the neurology sections of the Policlinic.

I had just left one sickroom and was about to enter the next, when a young nurse approached me. She asked, on behalf of her supervisor in Oral Surgery, if I could spare a bed from my department for a patient who had just had surgery. I agreed, and she left with a grateful smile. I turned to my assistant: "Did you see those eyes?"

1947. That nurse became my wife. Eleonore Katharina, née Schwindt.

Gabriele is our daughter, and our son-in-law is Franz Vesely, professor of physics at the University of Vienna. Katharina and Alexander are our grandchilden. All of us continue to live in Vienna.

Frankl's wife Elly, 1949.

Elly Frankl, 1964.

Frankl's daugher Gabriele and her (later) husband Franz Vesely, 1966.

Frankl's grandchildren Katharina and Alexander Vesely, representing their grandfather at the Ninth World Congress of Logotherapy in Toronto, 1993.

Endnotes

1. Oskar Wiener, born March 4, 1873, in Prague, deported April 20, 1944. Poet, writer, feuilletonist, and publisher (*Alt-Prager Guckkasten*).
2. Gustav Meyring, born January 19, 1868 in Vienna, died December 4, 1932, in Starnberg. Austrian Writer, contributor to *Simplicissimus*, author of fantasy novels in the style of E. T. A. Hoffmann and E. A. Poe. Best-known work: *Der Golem* (1915).
3. Rashi, born 1040 in Troyes, died 1105 in Troyes. Real name: Salomo ben Isaak; Jewish Bible and Talmud interpreter. Named after him is the Rashi script, a Hebraic square script used primarily in Bible and Talmud commentaries.
4. Maharal. "Ma Ha Ral" is the abbreviated form of the official title "Morenu H-rab Rabbenu" for Jehuda Ben Bezazel Löw (Rabbi Löw, popularly called "High Rabbi") which means "our teacher, our Rabbi Löw."
5. Joseph Maria von Bärnreither, born April 12, 1845, in Prague, died September 19, 1925 in Teplitz (now Czech Republic). Austrian politician, left historically valuable memoirs.
6. Styrian Autumn, (*Steirischer Herbst*) in Graz, Styria, cultural festival with exhibits, etc.
7. Paul Johannes Tillich, born August 20, 1886 in Starzeddel Germany, died October 22, 1965 in Chicago. American Protestant theologian of German origin, his main work, *Systematische Theologie,* created a comprehensive synthesis of theology and philosophy.
8. Juan Battista Torello, psychiatrist and Catholic priest residing in Vienna.
9. Rax, a plateau-type Alpine mountain, on the border between Lower Austria and Styria.
10. Viktor E. Frankl: *Ein Psycholog erlebt das Konzentrationslager [A Psychologist Experiences the Concentration Camp]*, pub-

lished in 1945 by Verlag für Jugend und Volk, Vienna. Later retitled...*trotzdem Ja zum Leben Sagen* [*Say Yes to Life in Spite of Everything*]. Many new editions. The English version bears the title *Man's Search for Meaning*.

11. Wilhelm Ostwald, born September 2, 1853, in Riga (now Latvia), died April 14, 1932, in Leipzig, Germany. Natural scientist and philosopher.

12. Gustav Theodor Fechner, born 1801 in Leipzig, died 1897 in Leipzig. Important proponent of experimental psychology.

13. Eduard Hirschmann, born July 28, 1871, in Vienna, died July 31, 1957, in Gloucester, Massachusetts. Austrian physician and psychoanalyst. Co-publisher of the *International Journal for Psychoanalysis*.

14. Paul Schilder, born February 15, 1886, in Vienna, died December 7, 1940, in New York. Austrian physician and psychoanalyst. Helped in the breakthrough of psychoanalysis in the United States.

15. Julius Ritter Wagner von Jauregg, born March 7, 1857, in Wels, Austria, died September 27, 1940, in Vienna. Nobel Prize for Medicine (1927) for infection therapy in psychoses.

16. Kurt R. Eissler, born 1908 in Vienna. Austrian psychologist and philosopher, founder of the Sigmund Freud archives in New York. Best-known work: the psychoanalytical study *Goethe* (1938).

17. Josef Gerstmann, born July 17, 1887, in Lemberg. Important Viennese neurologist, head of the mental hospital Maria Theresien Schlössel. Immigrated to the U.S., described the Gerstmann "angularis syndrome" (Agraphie, Akalkulie, and disturbance in the right–left orientation).

18. John Ruskin, born February 8, 1819, in London, died January 20, 1900, in Coniston, Cumbria, England. Writer, painter, and social philosopher, spokesman for social and political reforms.

19. Fritz Künkel, born September 6, 1889, in Stolzenburg (now Rumania), died April 4, 1956, in the U.S. Physician and psychotherapist, one of the prominent students of Alfred Adler.

20. Rudolf Allers and Oswald Schwarz, two prominent individual psychologists who left the Society for Individual Psychology where their anthropological viewpoint found no place.
21. Max Scheler, born August 22, 1874, in Munich, died May 19, 1928, in Frankfurt/Main. German philosopher. Founded a "material value ethics" and developed his own cultural sociology and a modern philosophical anthropology.
22. Erwin Wexberg, born February 12, 1889, in Vienna. Works on psychotherapy and neurology. Publications on individual psychology (*Individual Psychology: A Systematic Presentation*).
23. Rudolf Dreikurs, born February 8, 1874, in Vienna, died May 25, 1972, in Chicago. Austrian educator and psychologist. One of the most important representatives of individual psychology, he founded Adler institutes in Chicago, Rio de Janeiro, and Tel Aviv. Important works: *Children Challenge Us* and *Psychology in the Class Room*.
24. Fritz Wittels, born November 14, 1880, in Vienna, died October 16, 1950, in New York. Neurologist, psychiatrist, and psychoanalyst.
25. Fritz Redlich, born January 18, 1866, in Brünn (now Czech Republic), died June 9, 1930, in Vienna. The Redlich phenomenon of the eye (pupils) occurring with epilepsy and hysteria is named after him. Publications in all fields of neurology.
26. Peter Hofstätter, born October 20, 1913, died 1994 near Hamburg. In the early 1950s reintroduced experimental and empirical methods in German psychology (for instance, the polarity profile according to Osgood).
27. William Masters, born 1915, and Virginia Johnson, born 1925. American sex therapists.
28. Gordon W. Allport, born November 11, 1897, in Montezuma, Indiana, died October 19, 1967, in Cambridge, Massachusetts. American psychologist, who, with his works on personal development, laid the foundations of human-

istic psychology. Best-known work: *The Nature of Prejudice.*

29. Leopold Szondi, born November 3, 1893, in Neutra, Hungary, died in 1977. Hungarian psychologist and psychotherapist.

30. Ilse Aichinger, born November 1, 1921, in Vienna. Austrian writer.

31. August Aichhorn, born July 27, 1878, in Vienna, died October 13, 1949, in Vienna. Austrian educator and psychoanalyst. Founder of the Austrian psychoanalytical pedagogy, developed diagnostic and therapeutic methods for the resocializing of neglected children and delinquent youths.

32. Charlotte Bühler, born December 20, 1893, in Berlin, died February 2, 1974, in Stuttgart. German psychologist. In the 1930s she established a group of scientists doing research on child and youth psychology, the Viennese School, and made available development and intelligence tests.

33. Wilhelm Reich, born March 24, 1897, in Dobrzcynica (now Poland), died November 11, 1957, in Lewisburg, Pennsylvania. Austrian psychoanalyst. He tried to combine the theories of Marx and Freud and did biological-psychological research on fear and sexuality. Had strong influence on the anti-authoritarian movement of the sixties. Major works: *The Mass Psychology of Fascism* (1933), *Character Analysis* (1933), *The Sexual Revolution* (1945).

34. Otto Pötzl, born October 29, 1877, in Vienna, died April 1, 1962, in Vienna. Psychiatrist and neurologist, head of the Psychiatric Clinic of the University of Vienna. Was the first to introduce a course on psychoanalysis in the German-language area.

35. Corrugator phenomenon. Diagnostically useful phenomenon for suspected schizophrenia. First described by Frankl in the *Zeitschrift für Neurologie und Psychiatrie*, 1935 (vol. 15, p. 161f), with the title *A Frequent Phenomenon of Schizophrenia.*

36. Leopold Pawlicki, for many years head of Vienna's mental institution *Steinhof.* His son: Norbert Pawlicki, born March 4, 1923, in Vienna, died July 15, 1994, in Vienna. Pianist and composer.

37. Kurt Schuschnigg, born December 12, 1897, in Riva, Lake Garda (now Italy), died November 18, 1977, in Mutters near Innsbruck. Austrian politician and jurist. Was forced to resign as chancellor of Austria, March 11, 1938, under Nazi pressure.

38. Trepanieren (to trepan): operative opening of a medullary or cranulary cavity.

39. Dandy, American brain surgeon, working with Cushing, the founder of modern brain surgery, published a standard work on the subject.

40. Cardiazol shock, artificial induction of an epileptic attack, first suggested by Meduna.

41. Congress report, Strengholt, Amsterdam

42. From a letter by Professor Robert C. Barnes, president of the American Viktor Frankl Institute of Logotherapy and of the Tenth World Congress of Logotherapy (Dallas, Texas, 1995), I learned that he had "done research through the Pentagon in Washington, D.C., in an attempt to locate any survivors of the Army regiment from Texas that liberated you from the camp at Türkheim. Had you been able to be with us, we had hoped to encourage even a small reunion of those men with you at that time. We have been able to locate, and we have in our possession, a uniform worn by the second man through the gate on that memorable day. His widow has provided us with his army uniform. His name was Sgt. Barton T. Fuller." If I had not been prevented by sickness from attending the Congress, I would have fallen to my knees and kissed the uniform.

43. Martin Heidegger, born September 26, 1889, in Messkirch, Germany, died May 26, 1976, in Freiburg, Germany. Existential philosopher. Main work: *Sein und Zeit* [*Being and Time*], 1927. With his thoughts on questions of meaning he greatly influenced theology and psychology.

44. Ludwig Binswanger, born April 13, 1881, in Kreuzlingen, Switzerland, died February 5, 1966, in Kreuzlingen. Swiss psychiatrist, extended psychotherapy with the so-called *Daseinsanalyse* (existential analysis).
45. Karl Jaspers, born February 23, 1883, in Oldenburg, Germany, died February 26, 1969, in Basel, Switzerland. Main exponent of existential philosophy. Main works: *General Psychopathology* (1913); *Philosophy* (1932).
46. Gabriel Marcel, born December 12, 1889 in Paris, died October 18, 1973 in Paris. French philosopher and playwright.

Index

About Viktor Frankl

Viktor E. Frankl is professor of neurology and psychiatry at the University of Vienna. He has lectured around the world, and has held professorships also in the United States, at Harvard University in 1961, at Southern Methodist University in 1966, and at Duquesne University in 1972. The United States International University, San Diego, established for him in 1970 a chair in logotherapy, which is now known as "The Third Viennese School of Psychotherapy" (following Freud's psychoanalysis and Adler's individual psychology).

Frankl has received 28 honorary doctorates from universities around the world. Austria has conferred on him the highest honor of the Republic for scientific achievements, one with only 18 recipients. The Austrian Academy of Sciences has made him an honorary member.

For 25 years Frankl was chief in the neurology department of the Policlinic Hospital, Vienna.

He has written 32 books, some of which now appear in 24 translations, including Japanese, Chinese, Korean, and Russian. His *Man's Search for Meaning* has sold over nine million copies in the English editions alone. The United States Library of Congress has listed it as "one of the ten most influential books in America."

Other authors have written about Frankl and logotherapy in 145 books, 154 dissertations, and more than 1,400 articles in scientific journals.

He has lectured at the University of Vienna as recently as 1996.